For James and Charles

Contents

CONTENTS

Notes on the text

Notes on the Calendar

Before 1918 Russia followed the Julian Calendar, which, at the beginning of the twentieth century, was thirteen days behind the Gregorian Calendar. In February 1918, in the aftermath of the revolution, Russia formally adopted the Gregorian Calendar, the calendar used throughout Western Europe.

All dates relating to events that occurred in Russia before 1918, including those dates directly quoted from Henriette's memoir, correspond to the Julian Calendar. The only exceptions are those occasions when Henriette was either living or travelling in the West.

In addition, in the run-up to the Great War, where I have cited two dates (OS) signifies 'Old Style' and denotes the Julian Calendar.

Notes on Place Names

As far as possible I have endeavoured to employ those names currently in use at the time. To this end my copy of *Baedeker's Russia 1914* has proved an invaluable resource. Any errors are mine.

In the tsarist Russian provinces such as Courland, where Russian and German place names were generally interchangeable, I have used the more usual German rather than the Russian names. Where applicable I have also put the present-day Latvian names in brackets. In the chapter that covers the period between the wars, when Latvia was an independent country, all place names are given in Latvian.

I should add that, for the sake of clarity, I have anglicised the names of certain streets, buildings and other landmarks.

Notes on Russian Names

Although I have generally conformed to the conventions of modern usage, where I have quoted from works by other authors I have remained faithful to the original. As a result the spelling of individual names will inevitably vary.

To add to these inconsistencies, I have kept to the familiar English spellings of those writers, musicians, members of the imperial family and other Russian notables who are well-known in the West. Where I have retained Henriette's spelling, her versions of Schaliapin, Czar and Czaritsa are in fact consistent with contemporary usage.

Although most of the names of the notable Russians who appear within these pages have been anglicised over the years there have been a number of variations. For instance, at the beginning of the twentieth century, the American public knew the conductor Vasily Safonov as Wassily Safonoff.

CHAPTER 1

PRELUDE

Some forty years ago, my grandmother, Henriette, quietly handed me two plain red exercise books; to my surprise the narrowly ruled pages, penned in her distinctive looped handwriting, contained the short memoir she had been working on for several months. I have them before me now, those two somewhat faded books in which she so painstakingly recorded the more remarkable incidents in what she described as her 'rather unusual life'.

Henriette had always known that she had a story to tell. From her birth in 1893 into a prosperous merchant family in tsarist Russia to her experiences in Europe and further afield, she had lived through and on several occasions been caught up in some of the most momentous historical events of the first half of the twentieth century: the wars and revolutions, which would impact on her career, her ambitions and her relationships.

Fascinated and deeply moved by an account that unexpectedly revealed the hopes and aspirations of the young woman she had once been, of the talented mezzo-soprano who had attempted to realise her ambitions within the constraints of marriage, motherhood and the chaos of political upheaval, I was also immensely grateful that she had been able to recollect so much. Then, fully occupied by my two small sons, I put both books carefully away in a drawer.

It was only in the 1990s that the fall of the Iron Curtain, together with the expansion of the Internet and the greater accessibility of archival resources, encouraged me to look at her memoir again. When I came to do so I soon realised that in order to fully appreciate her experiences, to do justice to her account, I would need to approach the task from a historical perspective. With this objective in mind I resolved not only to research the background against which she had played out her early life, to read newspapers and other contemporary reports but also, wherever possible, to visit the most relevant locations.

Over the last few years I have embarked on a journey that has amounted to something of a pilgrimage. By venturing to many of the towns, cities and countries that made up Henriette's world, by endeavouring to see beyond the physical as well as the political changes that have inevitably befallen them, I have tried to imagine them as they might have been in the first decades of the twentieth century. It is an approach that has enabled me to travel in my mind's eye from tsarist Russia to suffragist Edinburgh, from revolutionary Moscow to peacetime Latvia, from Weimar Berlin to post-war New York. In doing so I have been able to gain a better understanding of Henriette's story.

However, while Henriette's narrative inevitably takes centre stage, other voices also play their part. Her friend and teacher the Russian singer Anna El-Tour, her mentor and accompanist Coenraad V. Bos, the conductor Arthur Nikisch and the great Russian basso Feodor Chaliapin are among a number of musicians who put in an appearance. And, indeed, it is the collective observations of those writers, musicians and other contemporaries who shared her experiences that place the events that shaped and deflected her life in a wider context and give a greater insight into the geopolitical and cultural world in which she lived.

I have come to admire not only the way in which she confronted some of the issues of her time, but also the courage she exhibited as she reacted to and coped with the vagaries of history, the unforeseen events over which she had no control. The changing role of women, the difficulties involved in combining marriage with a career and the displacements occasioned by loss of home and country still resonate in today's uncertain climate.

Although I was always extremely close to her, Henriette was a very private person. She rarely spoke about the past. Her memoirs were a revelation to me and my only regret is that it was my mother Tatiana's untimely death that proved to be the catalyst, and no doubt the inspiration, for her endeavour. But now, after so many years, what for Henriette was undoubtedly a cathartic process, has become for me a voyage of discovery and, I hope, a tribute to my beloved grandmother.

CHAPTER 2

OVERTURE

One morning, towards the end of the summer of 1903, sharp-eyed readers of *The Times* Court Circular column might have noticed the following brief announcement:

> The Tsar and Tsaritsa and the Empress Alexander left St. Petersburg for Libau yesterday.[1]

Two days later, on 23 August 1903, Nicholas II arrived in Libau. He had come to visit the great naval fortress, a vast complex of dockyards and batteries, barracks and workshops where, it was reported, he would 'consecrate a new church' and 'inspect the naval dockyards' presently 'in the course of completion'.[2] Some two years earlier the Tsar had travelled to Libau, one of the bases of the Baltic Fleet, in order to witness the consecration of the cornerstone of the St Nicholas Maritime Cathedral. This time, accompanied by his wife Alexandra, he would attend a service in the recently completed cathedral, a large and ornate Orthodox church, its five great onion domes each surmounted by a cross.

The imperial couple had agreed to combine this engagement with an official visit to the nearby town. And Libau, a prosperous and thriving maritime centre on Russia's Baltic coast, was determined to receive the imperial family in style: flags were flown, flowers banked up, trees planted in decorative pots and at least one temporary pavilion was erected, a tall and airy structure, with a preponderance of glass (not unlike a conservatory), which would have been very much in keeping with the town's role as a fashionable summer resort and watering-place.

Henriette, who was ten years old at the time, still vividly remembered the occasion:

> There were great preparations in the town to receive the Czar and Czaritsa for a visit to the fleet. A beautiful veranda was built in a park and they came to meet some of the children from our school. We were chosen and arranged in three rows and had to throw flowers while they were passing. They also spoke a few words to some of us. It was terribly exciting to be spoken to by the Czaritsa and I thought that I should never forget it.

As a young schoolgirl, standing in line with her fellow pupils, delighted and honoured to have been chosen to greet Nicholas and Alexandra, Henriette would no doubt have been overwhelmed by the magnificence of it all, by the Tsar, resplendent in his high-collared naval uniform, by Alexandra, elegant in a long white outfit complemented by a stylish hat. Henriette too would have been well turned out, in her best school uniform ('brown dresses and black pinafores for school, and a white pinafore for special occasions'), her hair neatly tied back:

> But the end of the day was not so happy. That night the building was burnt down and the next day the Cossacks were brought in. They rode the streets with

their sabres drawn and just killed anybody who dared to go out, especially in the workmen's quarter. No more than three people were allowed to be together. We were afraid to go home from school and stayed the night there, until peace was restored.

Some seventy-five years later, Henriette recognised that the events of that eagerly anticipated day had not only marked the end of her hitherto safe and secure childhood but had also foreshadowed the turbulent years that lay ahead. Within eighteen months the Cossacks, the Tsar's loyal cavalry, would unsheathe their sabres and rampage through the very heart of St Petersburg; the shock waves that followed the infamous violence of 'Bloody Sunday' would reverberate throughout the Russian Empire.

CHAPTER 3

LIBAU

Libau, Liepāja, Libava – three names, one town, the town on the Baltic coast where my grandmother, Henriette, was born. Three names that reflected the diverse character of the place with its population of Baltic Germans, Letts and Russians. The descendants of conquering Teutonic Knights and Russian invaders, they personified the unusual history of this tsarist Russian province and former Duchy of Courland.

Henriette always retained a nostalgic affection for the Libau of her childhood, for the long sandy beach, the invigoratingly cold sea, the parks, the dunes and the smell of the pine trees. But by the time her own grandchildren were born, the town where she had been brought up and where she had once been so happy was firmly immured behind the Iron Curtain. So for me, Libau, as she always called it, seemed to be a mythical place, never to be visited, forever inaccessible. It was only in the 1990s that I realised that I would at last be able to venture to the town where my grandmother had spent her childhood. I could now travel to a newly liberated Latvia and, while attempting to turn back the clock, I would try to breathe life into her memories.

Libau had long attracted merchants and traders. Ships had come to load and unload their wares at the quaysides, which were lined with wooden warehouses, in places two rows deep. In the nearby roads, the merchants had built their houses, first of wood and later of stone. Later on, when the river had silted up, threatening the town's status as a maritime trading centre, a new channel had been dug out in order to safeguard the harbour. By the end of the eighteenth century, Libau and Courland had become part of the Russian Empire.

I would find that, at the beginning of the twentieth century, this ice-free harbour on the Baltic Sea was not only one of Russia's largest ports but also a thriving commercial centre. Libau's relatively recent expansion had to a great extent been due to a marked improvement in communications with the Russian interior: in the second half of the nineteenth century the inauguration of new railway lines had enabled more goods to be transported. Trade had flourished and as a result the town had become increasingly prosperous.

Libau, or Liepāja as it is now called, boasts two distinctive buildings that date from the early days of this unprecedented prosperity: the Customs House and the Railway Station. These two imposing classical structures, both erected in the 1870s, clearly emphasise the importance that the railway and the harbour held and would continue to hold for the town's status as a trading centre.

Libau's rapid expansion had heralded a wave of new building. Many public edifices and large private residences were constructed: the Nikolai Gymnasium (the boys' school), the Hotel de Rome, the Merchants' Guild House, their red-brick façades punctuated by lavish classical details, all typify the 1880s. In the hitherto undeveloped seaside area, a park was laid out behind the sand dunes; villas and summer-houses were put up and Libau soon became a summer resort.

In the 1880s this thriving, bustling town would have attracted ambitious and energetic young men, men who welcomed the opportunity to prosper, men like Henriette's father. It was here that, either through luck or perspicacity, my great-grandfather had entered the timber trade, a rapidly developing industry. By the late 1890s, he was already a partner in a firm of timber merchants with an office in Libau's main street, the Grosse Strasse (I have used the German as opposed to the Russian name). A successful man, he would in due course have his own business.

Throughout Henriette's childhood Libau had been growing ever more rapidly. From some ten thousand inhabitants in 1863 to about thirty thousand in 1881, the population explosion had escalated unabated. By 1911, the year of her eighteenth birthday, the town would have over eighty thousand residents.[1] Factories, offices and housing for workers were built on the outskirts; in the centre a multitude of buildings exhibited the latest architectural styles: Art Nouveau, Eclectic and National Romantic.

Visiting Liepāja for the first time in 2001, I was delighted to find that so many of these buildings were still standing, albeit often in a state of disrepair, their ornamentation slowly crumbling. As I began to walk through the streets of the old town, trying to look at it through Henriette's eyes, the Libau of the 1890s and the 1900s gradually came to life again. I was glad that I was able to see beyond the run-down buildings with their faded façades to the dynamic town that Libau had once been, the Libau where Henriette had grown up.

The old building where Henriette's father once had his office is still there; a prestigious location, which was also conveniently close to the port and the sawmills. Grosse Strasse (now Liela iela) led to one of Libau's principal market squares, the Neuer Markt.

The Neuer Markt would function as an open market until about 1910 when it was replaced by an enormous public rose garden, and duly renamed Rosenplatz (Rožu laukums). Libau's other large market square was also the town's oldest: the Alter Markt Platz (Kuršu laukums). There were other smaller markets too, such as the Hay Market, where straw and hay and firewood could be purchased. These squares, which would once have been among the town's focal points, have survived as open spaces, and so it is not difficult to imagine them as they would have been at the turn of the century, with their bustling crowds and colourful stalls laden with all manner of produce. These were the markets of Henriette's childhood; it was only in 1910 that a large indoor market was erected beside the Old Market Square – the Alter Markt Platz.[2]

Many of the town's places of worship were built near the Alter Markt Platz. And, with one exception, they are all there today: St Ann's Lutheran Church, St Joseph's Roman Catholic Cathedral, St Paul's Baptist Church. Only the Jewish Synagogue in Peter Strasse has gone, destroyed in 1941.

It is only a few steps to Peldu iela (once Bade Strasse). An old postcard from the turn of the century shows a tree-lined street, horse-drawn open carriages and two large, attractive villas. This is the beginning of the seaside area. Grand houses, mostly dating from the 1890s and the early 1900s, border the streets on the eastern side of the park: wooden houses embellished with ornamental woodcuts; stone houses decorated with elaborate plasterwork; houses with gable-roofs, turrets, terraces, balconies and verandas. Set in fairly uniform plots and conforming to prescribed building rules, each house, whether of wooden or stone construction, gives the pleasing impression of being entirely different from its neighbours.

Bade Strasse led directly to the Bath House, the Nikolaibad. A low building with a Doric colonnade and a central cupola, it is now one of the few survivors of this once-fashionable watering-place. Another postcard: ladies in long dresses, parasols raised against the sun, a profusion of trees and, at the end of the path, a tiny temple. The photographer has positioned himself with his back to the Bath House in order to show the vista down to the Swan Pond. In the centre of the picture, a small temple stands on a minute island, its Doric columns and domed roof echoing the Bath House, which was also constructed in 1902. A hundred years later, the temple on the island has become something of an iconic image; and there are still swans in the circular pond.

Trees everywhere: linden, maple, willow, birch, fir, pine, all planted as the park was laid out. Across the ridge of sand dunes lies the long beach with its fine white sand. And then there is the sea. As a child Henriette would have come here to bathe and to collect pieces of golden amber from the Baltic Sea.

She must often have walked along Kurhaus Prospekt (Kūrmājas prospekts), which was a popular place for promenades: a wide tree-lined street, which even today has the appearance of a boulevard. A tram once ran here, past the offices of the East Asian Steamship Company, past the solid and imposing houses where some of the town's wealthiest merchants and traders lived, taking visitors directly from the station to the Kurhaus in the seaside park. They had come to Libau to take the baths: medicinal baths, warm sea-water baths, mud baths. But the Kurhaus, with its elegant restaurant and its garden where concerts were held daily in the summer, has long since gone; so too have the Herrenbad and the Damenbad, the wooden huts on stilts, which were segregated sea-bathing places for ladies and gentlemen.

Walking through the seaside park, looking for those long-vanished buildings, I came across a rough, grey, upright stone bearing the date 1905. It was a timely reminder that life in Libau had not always been as idyllically peaceful as I had begun to imagine.

There had, of course, been the alarming incident that had taken place just after Nicholas and Alexandra's official visit to the town. For Henriette, this would have been her first experience of violence, the first time that she would have been forced to confront the reality of what was happening in the world outside her family. As a young child she would doubtless have been unaware of the mounting tension and revolutionary unrest, the ongoing dissatisfaction with Nicholas II's policy of Russification and the widely held grievances against the Baltic German landowners.

But dissatisfaction with the Tsar's autocratic rule was by no means confined to Russia's Baltic provinces: with widespread unrest throughout the whole of the Russian Empire, the army, as the historian Orlando Figes has confirmed, had increasingly been called on to quell civilian dissension. In the decade preceding 1903, tsarist troops had already intervened over a thousand times.[3] Henriette's vivid recollection of the arson attack in Libau and the ensuing repercussions was an example of just such an instance: '…the next day the Cossacks were brought in. They rode the streets with their sabres drawn and just killed anybody who dared to go out and especially in the workmen's quarter'. It is not surprising that this incident, which took place in the summer of 1903, should have left such a lasting impression on her.

The following year, 1904, began inauspiciously: at the end of January, the Japanese attacked Russia's First Pacific Squadron, which was anchored at Port Arthur in Manchuria; an aggressive action that inaugurated the Russo-Japanese War of 1904–1905. The naval reinforcements that were urgently needed for the relief of Port Arthur meant that the Baltic Fleet, also known as the Second Pacific Squadron, would have to be prepared and equipped. In August 1904, the first ships were duly inspected by the Tsar at Cronstadt. Three days later they sailed for Reval (Tallinn), where they were joined by another group of ships and, at the end of September, the Tsar again inspected the squadron. The next day they left for Libau, the last port of call in Russia.

The arrival of the fleet, steaming majestically towards the naval harbour, would have been an impressive sight; only a few days later, on 2 October 1904, Henriette would have been able to watch the ships when they finally set out for the Far East, a journey that would take them half way round the world. In November, a few more hastily prepared ships would leave Libau and a further squadron, the Third Pacific Squadron, would set out from the naval harbour on 2 February 1905. It proved to be an ill-fated voyage: when the Baltic Fleet finally reached the Far East in May 1905, they would be crushingly defeated at the Battle of Tsushima.[4]

While the Tsar was persuaded to put an end to what had become a deeply unpopular war by agreeing to negotiate peace with Japan, at home revolutionary turmoil was already spreading relentlessly across the Russian Empire.[5] All this rebellious activity had been ignited by the cataclysmic events that had taken place in St Petersburg at the beginning of the year. On Sunday 9 January 1905, over a hundred thousand workers gathered together with the intention of delivering a petition to the Tsar. Led by Father Gapon, a priest sympathetic to their cause, they began marching peacefully towards the Winter Palace. Although many of the marchers were carrying icons and church banners, to the immense horror of all those who witnessed the occasion, they came under brutal attack from the tsarist troops who had lain in wait for them. Infantry, cavalry and mounted Cossacks equipped with sabres ruthlessly attempted to prevent the workers from reaching their destination. Men, women and children were attacked indiscriminately. Those who managed to reach the Palace Square were met with rifle fire. There were many casualties among the defenceless crowd.[6]

Appalling images of crimson-stained snow only added to the horrors of the day. While the *Times* correspondent was struck by '...the snow on the streets and pavements soaked with blood...',[7] the writer Maxim Gorky, who witnessed a cavalry attack on the Nevsky Prospekt, was shocked by the gratuitous brutality which saw 'a mounted soldier fire at a man who had already fallen to the ground'.[8] This fateful day, which inaugurated the 1905 Revolution and culminated in the downfall of the Romanov dynasty, would come to be known as 'Bloody Sunday'.

In the days and weeks following 'Bloody Sunday', strikes and demonstrations erupted throughout the Russian Empire, including the cities of the Baltic provinces.[9] When thousands of protesting workers marched through the streets of Riga on 13 January, the Russian Governor-General had responded swiftly and brutally, ordering his troops to open fire on the demonstrators. Some fifty civilians would be killed that day, with two hundred more reputed to have been wounded.[10]

A few days later, Cossack troops attacked workers in Libau. Looking at the stone, which I had so inadvertently discovered in the beautiful seaside park, I now realised that it had been placed there to commemorate this violent incident. The brief engraved inscription not only highlighted the date (16 January 1905) but also made it clear that the stone was intended to serve as a memorial to those workers who had been "massacred" that day.

Outbreaks of strikes and violence continued to punctuate life in Libau throughout 1905. The trouble would also spread to the nearby countryside where estates were attacked and property was seized and sometimes vandalised. So extensive was the damage that it has been suggested that as many as forty Baltic German manor houses were burned in Courland alone.[11] Despite the fact that martial law had been declared in the province in August that year, the looting and arson persisted throughout the winter of 1905–1906, a period that saw a repressive six-month campaign of punitive reprisals, with tsarist troops being repeatedly called in to quell the ongoing violence.[12]

The disruption was not confined to the Baltic provinces. From Odessa to Moscow, from Riga to St Petersburg, there was widespread anger and insurrection. In the autumn of 1905, Russia was paralysed by a general strike and the Tsar reluctantly signed the October Manifesto. But by the following spring Nicholas had broken his word: by restricting the already limited powers of the Duma he had gone back on his previous assurances.[13] To all intents and purposes the Revolution of 1905 was only a dress rehearsal; the real drama would not be enacted for another decade.

15

CHAPTER 4

AN EDUCATION

Henriette rarely spoke about her childhood. We were aware that she was the elder daughter of a wealthy timber merchant, the second of his four children, and that she had enjoyed a comfortable and privileged upbringing. We understood that she had both loved and admired her parents, her father with his boundless generosity and her mother who she would later describe as 'young and beautiful'; and we knew that she had grown up in a stable and secure environment: 'We were a very happy family and I had an elder brother by two and a half years. Later on I had another brother and sister'. As children we were intrigued when she described her elder brother with his fair hair and blue eyes, or her younger red-headed sister, and even more so when we learnt that her own hair had been so dark that it was almost blue-black. And we were delighted when she conjured up dunes and pine trees and long white sandy beaches where an exotic gem called amber was washed ashore by an unfamiliar Baltic Sea.

But almost three-quarters of a century later, when she came to write her memoirs, she would write surprisingly little about those early years or even, indeed, about her family. She would instead confine herself to writing an account of her own experiences, of her memories of particular events and people and the impact they had on her career, her ambitions and her personal life: a highly selective approach, which I have felt bound both to follow and to respect.

We always knew that Henriette came from a cultured family. 'On my sixth birthday', she wrote, 'I got a Steinway piano and started my first music lessons. My father loved music and even my first exercises filled him with joy. These music lessons continued for a long time and I cannot remember a day when I did not practise for one hour the piano'. A present that, by inspiring and fostering her lifelong love of music, would come to drive her aims and ambitions for the next forty years. And a present that also exemplified my great-grandfather's serious and disciplined approach as well as his characteristic generosity.

A year or so later, Henriette would once again endeavour to fulfil her father's expectations: 'When I was seven and a half I had to pass an entrance examination to a *gymnasium* (school) which was under the auspices of the Czar's mother. It was very important to get into this school, as that was the best education you could get'. These gymnasia or girls' day schools did indeed offer the best education in Russia: by completing the full curriculum and successfully passing the rigorous final examinations, students were able to gain admittance to a university. 'Our course lasted eight years', she explained, 'first the preparatory class and then seven more real classes. We had many subjects, much more than any other school. It was a very strict school, but nevertheless we were all quite happy'.

Although the Revolution of 1905 had effectively ensured that life in Libau would never be quite the same again – as Henriette remarked, 'an uneasy feeling prevailed for some time'– she was more concerned with finishing her education, passing the final examinations and gaining the coveted diploma:

> I must mention some of our examinations, for they still haunt me sometimes. The first exam was a Russian essay and we were given six hours to write. I cannot forget how upset I was when I read that we had to write about the importance of the Stone Ghost [sic], the statue overlooking the Neva in St Petersburg. We had never discussed this subject and what can one write on such an abstract theme? By the end of six hours our papers were taken. I had written two large pages and that was all, bringing in history and whatever I could think of. I went home and decided that I had failed and would not be allowed to continue with the rest of the papers.

To her relief, she 'was given a pass and could go on to the most difficult subjects'. There then followed several weeks of further examinations. In every discipline, whether Russian, French, German or history, there was 'the same procedure: first the essay and then the oral, but the worst was the mathematics, algebra and geometry and that', Henriette recalled, 'was my last dreadful experience. It was my last examination and there was one theory that I could not understand. It was Pythagorean, or something like that. My teacher started with it and I told him I could not do it and would he ask any other questions, which I could answer. He kept me for a long time explaining it to me and then decided I could not have my diploma without the proper knowledge. I was getting quite faint and at the end collapsed. Luckily', she added, 'I did not have any weak marks in other subjects so they had to give me my diploma'.

Only recently, on a visit to Russia, I came across just such a diploma, displayed behind glass in the showcase of a museum. Entitled *ATTESTATS* (the capital letters strikingly picked out in gold) and surrounded by a gold framework incorporating the Romanov double-headed imperial eagle, this large and impressive certificate had become a relic of a by-gone age.

Henriette's immediate ambition was to carry on with her musical education and become a pianist. Her father, however, had other ideas: 'He was a great admirer of England and he decided that I must first take a degree at an English university and then devote my life to music'. Having made sure that she was fluent in both Russian and German – 'We had a German governess and so we spoke at home two languages' – he was adamant that she should become proficient in English. She was given no choice: 'As a father he was very strict with us and we had to obey all his wishes. We all had to learn English'. In the event, she would attend a Scottish university.

CHAPTER 5

EDINBURGH

In the autumn of 1909, Henriette left Libau for the first time. She travelled with her father across Europe, to Scotland, which was one of his principal export markets. It would appear that when it came to choosing a university for his elder daughter my great-grandfather had turned to his connections in the timber trade and, as a child of the 1890s, my grandmother would never have considered disobeying her father's wishes. But it must have been an unnerving proposition:

> I was just sixteen and had never been away from home. It was a great ordeal for me to be separated from my mother. I did not know any English but my father had arranged everything very well. I was admitted to Masson Hall [the women's hall of residence] at George Square.

Edinburgh was an enlightened choice. Women had first been admitted to the university as undergraduates in 1892, considerably earlier than their Russian counterparts. By the second half of the nineteenth century, Ladies' Educational Associations dedicated to providing lectures for women looking for academic instruction were already flourishing in cities such as Manchester, Liverpool and Leeds.[1] North of the Border, the Edinburgh Ladies' Educational

Association (the precursor of the Edinburgh Association for the University Education of Women) had first been established in 1867.[2] And in fact it was largely due to the efforts of its successor, the EAUEW, as well as to professors such as David Masson and Gerard Baldwin Brown, who not only lectured extensively at university level to their members but also firmly supported their objectives, that women had been accepted as students of the university.

Frances Helen Simson, who graduated from Edinburgh University in 1893, had for a time attended classes run by the EAUEW. One of the university's first eight women graduates, she had remained closely involved with the Association and when Masson Hall, the university's hall of residence for women students, was formally opened in November 1897, she became its first warden.[3]

The impetus behind the foundation of the Hall (named after Professor Masson) had initially come from the Association, which was instrumental in launching an appeal to raise money for 'a Hall of Residence and a Library, to serve as a meeting-place for rest and study for all matriculated women students'.[4] Subscriptions were duly solicited and received, primarily from local donors. One noteworthy exception was a donation of £5 from Miss Emily Davies, the distinguished founder of Girton College, Cambridge, and a tireless promoter of higher education for women.

The building chosen for the new hall of residence was 31 George Square, on the edge of Edinburgh's Old Town. It was an eminently desirable location. 'The front windows look out on the large garden in the centre of the Square', enthused an early prospectus, 'the back windows command a view of the Meadows [the extensive park directly behind the house]; Blackford and Braid Hills; and the Pentlands.

21

George Square, although it is within a few minutes walk of the University and close to busy thoroughfares, is itself free from noise and traffic, and an air of old-world dignity seems to pervade it'.[5]

After the necessary alterations, which included 'the installation of the electric light' and the construction of a dining-room, the Hall would be able to accommodate some fifteen students, each with their own separate bedroom or study-bedroom. The hope was expressed that Masson Hall would emulate the Oxford women's colleges, which had opened a decade or so earlier, by becoming 'like Somerville, Lady Margaret's and St Hughes at Oxford'.[6]

A number of rooms were also set aside for the use of non-resident women students, who would be required to pay a small fee for this privilege. While Masson Hall would serve as 'a meeting-place for non-resident women students', who were entitled 'to have Lunch or Tea in the Hall at a reasonable fixed rate of charge', the first floor drawing-room, which occupied the full width of the house, was reserved for the small number of women who lived in the Hall and had their bedrooms on the upper floors of the building. These students, the prospectus pointed out, 'have the use of the books in the library gratis, as well as of the lighter literature to be found on the drawing-room shelves'. Prospective residents were assured that 'The furnishings of the house and its pretty and suitable appointments speak for themselves of the care and taste that have been expended on its interior arrangements'.[7]

Four photographs still survive from those early days. Dating from about 1900, these evocative black-and-white images are carefully preserved in the University of Edinburgh's Archives.

The only exterior view reveals the entrance to an eighteenth-century Georgian building, the front door flanked by two Doric columns decorated in the neo-classical style which was so characteristic of the second half of the century, the period when the houses in George Square were originally constructed on land just to the south of the Old Town. A brass nameplate confirms that this is indeed MASSON HALL and, lest we be in any doubt, the number 31 is inscribed on the glass panel above the door.

The remaining photographs all illustrate interior views. There is a large reception room, still with the original eighteenth-century chimney-piece and cornice, light and delicate in the manner of Robert Adam. But the room has recently been decorated: the walls have been hung with a densely patterned paper, a flowered rug has been laid on the floor and flower-filled vases and potted palms are displayed on the tables, all in the best late-Victorian tradition. The Pfeiffer Room (named after a generous benefactor) has been decorated in a similar fashion although, in this case, glass-fronted bookcases line the walls and low-hanging pendant lights illuminate the rather more utilitarian tables and chairs.

Another image shows a student's study-bedroom: the iron bed is covered with an Indian bedspread, a patterned rug lies on the floor and the walls are papered with a print reminiscent of the work of William Morris. A mirror stands on top of the plain chest-of-drawers and a comfortable wicker armchair with a cushion has been placed near the window. A table, together with two rush-seated chairs and a small hanging bookshelf complete the furnishings of the room. A lamp hangs from a cord in the ceiling (electric lighting was initially only available until about 11 o'clock at night) and a kettle and a coal-scuttle sit on the floor next to the recently installed fireplace – fires were generally provided at a small extra charge.

Years later, in her semi-autobiographical novel *Making Conversation*, the writer Christine Longford, who first went up to Oxford in 1918, would describe a room in an Oxford women's college: 'It contained an iron bed with an Indian printed bed-spread; a chest-of-drawers with a small mirror hanging on a nail above it; a table and a small chair; a big basket-chair by the fireplace... The floor was stained, with a rug in the middle'.[8] A room in which the Masson Hall student of 1900 would no doubt have felt very much at home.

Within a decade Masson Hall would be in a position to accommodate several more students. In fact the enlargement of the Hall through the acquisition of an adjacent building (32 George Square) and the subsequent alterations would more or less have coincided with Henriette's arrival in Edinburgh in the autumn of 1909.

Henriette and her father had travelled by train, from Libau to Berlin and then west through Germany. A novel experience: the Russian guards, 'black blouse' belted at the waist, 'wide trousers tucked into the boots, and a round fur cap',[9] the frontier station at Verzhbolovo (Wirballen), the last station in the Russian Empire; the final glimpse of Russia; the sleeping-car; the arrival in Berlin – a journey of some twenty-four hours in all. Then, perhaps, the *Nord Express*, which operated daily between Berlin and London's Charing Cross Station, running via Hanover, Cologne and Brussels before arriving at Ostend and the awaiting cross-channel steamer; this was the fastest and most convenient route to England.

While the entire trip to London could have been accomplished in under two days, Henriette's father chose to break the journey in the German capital. They went shopping:

> The trouble was that during my school years we had to wear uniform: brown dresses and black pinafores for school, and a white pinafore for special occasions. I did not have any other clothes, so my father bought a whole suitcase of clothes in Berlin on our way to Edinburgh. We got all the wrong things, especially a hat that was so big that one could not go through a door...

At the time these gigantic hats – some extravagantly tall, others impossibly wide – were all the rage. But, however fashionable they may have been, they were obviously not appropriate for a sixteen-year-old girl.

When they finally reached Masson Hall, the maid who unpacked Henriette's suitcase was so shocked to find these flamboyant clothes that she immediately 'told Miss Simson they were not suitable'. The wise and compassionate Frances Simson promptly took matters in hand and ordered what Henriette would later describe as 'some proper suits'– a tailored longish coat and matching ankle-length skirt – 'to wear at the University and also for going out to visit people'. A high-necked blouse and, much to her dismay, 'shoes with low heels which were very uncomfortable' would have completed her outfit.

Frances Simson now showed great kindness towards the young girl who had been put into her charge and for whom she must have felt particularly responsible. 'At first', Henriette wrote, 'Miss Simson did not let me go out by myself and accompanied me to my music lessons. I must also mention', she added, 'that from the first day of my stay a piano was hired for me and put in the basement, where we had our meals. I was to practice from eleven to one o'clock when the students were mostly away'.

There is no doubt that Frances Simson was an exceptional woman who not only had a profound influence on Henriette but also on all those with whom she came into contact. The appreciation of her life that was published in the *Masson Association News Letter* of 1938 described how when Miss Simson had first been put in charge of Masson Hall she had attempted to model it 'as far as possible upon the home in which she herself had been brought up' so that from its very beginning the Hall 'had stamped upon it a peculiar and individual charm'. It was the 'respect and affection inspired by Miss Simson [that] furnished the unifying principle' of the Hall. 'She never formulated a rule, nor gave an order; the wishes she expressed bore no relation to her own comfort and convenience; and it was felt to be unpardonable to do anything that might distress her'. 'Masson', the writer concluded, 'was built up round her unselfishness, her strength, her sanity'.[10] As a young and impressionable girl, Henriette would have respected and been inspired by Miss Simson's quiet perseverance and fortitude, her firm belief in the work ethic and her courage.

'So many memory-pictures come crowding up as one looks back', the *News Letter* recollected: 'Miss Simson comforting an Honours finalist with hot soup in the small hours of the morning...Miss Simson in fancy-dress, taking part in some ridiculous end of term orgy for which no costume might cost more than 1s. 6d.; or intimating with a twinkle in her eye, that Pfeiffer Room rugs would last longer if not used as toboggans'.[11] How Henriette would have valued her humanity and how she must have loved her sense of fun!

In addition to her academic distinction and her role in promoting the higher education of women, Frances Simson was a notable suffragist, committed to a non-militant approach. She had been one of the original members of the Women Graduates of Scottish Universities (Parliamentary Franchise) Committee when it was formed in 1906. These women, who were all members of the General Council of Edinburgh University, had attracted a measure of notoriety when, on being denied the right to vote for the University's Member of Parliament, they had decided to address the issue by taking legal action.[12] Their argument centred on a technicality, namely that the wording of the Representation of the People (Scotland) Act of 1868 relating to the franchise for Scottish universities had specifically referred to a "Person" or "Persons",[13] and it was on these grounds that, in the autumn of 1908, they proceeded to take their case all the way to the House of Lords; an action which had been fully supported by Frances Simson who, together with Chrystal Macmillan, had put the case for the appellants.[14]

Personally, I find it hard to imagine how difficult it must have been for Henriette to adapt to this unfamiliar environment and she never forgot those 'first few weeks, when I could not say a word'. A daunting experience, but one that would encourage her to be self-reliant, a capability that would only too soon prove invaluable. 'I had to get used to everything', she recalled, 'and I think that was the best thing that could happen to me and that helped me in my future life'.

If Miss Simson had been startled by Henriette's inappropriate wardrobe, Henriette herself had been equally unimpressed by her first encounter with her fellow students. 'I was very surprised', she confessed, 'when I saw that they were all wearing glasses'; an evocative comment that succinctly conjures up the image of a bevy of bluestockings, and an observation that will be echoed by Martha, the heroine of Christine Longford's previously mentioned novel, *Making Conversation*. It is Martha who humorously draws our attention to the 'woman in navy-blue silk with hair in plaits round her head and rimless eyeglasses'[15] who she finds in her room on her first night at Oxford; later that evening, to her amusement, 'another knock at the door' heralds the arrival of 'another girl with rimless eyeglasses'.[16]

Despite Henriette's somewhat dramatic arrival and her initial surprise at seeing so many bespectacled young women, it would not be long before she began to enjoy life at Masson Hall:

> We were only eighteen students at that time and it was very elegant. We had several Reception rooms, only single rooms and good [maid] service... I made some good friends, after their first shock at seeing somebody from Russia. The first question was, 'Do bears walk in the streets?' and other questions which they must have read in some fairy tales.

Frances Simson had arranged for Henriette to be taught English by a young woman called Leo Bennet – 'Her father was a Judge but when he died apparently he did not leave much money and they were five sisters'. They followed a strict schedule: 'I learned one hundred words every day and then forgot them, but at the end they all came back and I had a good vocabulary'. Leo Bennet was also 'very particular about the pronunciation, and we worked before a mirror', practising the unfamiliar vowels and consonants. The two women became great friends and Henriette would often visit her home.

In the autumn of 1910, by which time she was more or less fluent in English, Henriette was permitted to enter the university. She would be among the many students, both male and female, who, even though they did not intend to graduate, were allowed to follow classes on payment of a matriculation fee (one guinea for the academic year) and the relevant class fees. Exempt from having to pass the university's preliminary examination, she would simply have had to sign the First Matriculation Book and purchase a class ticket for each course of lectures she proposed to attend.

Henriette had chosen to follow courses in Political Economy and Fine Art. However, while the former seems to have made little impression on her, she enthusiastically attended the classes given by the renowned Professor of Fine Art, Gerard Baldwin Brown. An eminent art historian, Professor Baldwin Brown had first been appointed to the recently created Watson-Gordon Chair of Fine Art in 1880, when he was just over thirty years old; it was a position he would hold for the next fifty years.

Throughout his long career Gerard Baldwin Brown published extensively. His oeuvres included a six-volume survey of the *Arts in Early England*, monographs on *William Hogarth* and *Rembrandt* and numerous other publications and articles. His book *The Fine Arts: A Manual*, which first came out in 1891, would eventually run to four editions. Dealing with the 'arts of form…the so-called fine arts of

Architecture, Sculpture and Painting', this comprehen
sive work exemplifies Professor Baldwin Brown's scholarly
approach to his discipline.

A remarkable academic, he was also by all accounts an
unusually sympathetic man and when confronted by the
young Russian girl in his class he had immediately gone
out of his way to make her feel at home. She was invited
to breakfast parties at his house in George Square: 'The
Professor', she wrote, 'used to have the most extraordinary
people from different countries. The first time I was asked
to assist at a breakfast party I was very excited to follow
the English style of breakfast and did my best'.

Little did she know that these parties would one day
become legendary. Some twenty years later, when Professor
Baldwin Brown stepped down from the Chair of Fine
Art, he was the subject of an article which appeared in the
Edinburgh University Journal of 1930. Written by one of
his former students to mark the fiftieth anniversary of his
professorship, the article recounted how he took '...a practical interest in his class, which showed itself for example
in his breakfast parties at the beginning of the session, at
which he wished his students to meet in another atmosphere
than that of the lecture-room, and to realise that the pursuit
of culture belonged to the whole of life, as much to social
intercourse as to the cramming of facts'.[17]

Henriette gratefully accepted the Baldwin Browns' hospi-
tality on a number of other occasions and she was delighted
when, that year, they asked her to have 'Christmas Dinner
with them'. The couple lived at 50 George Square, which
was on the east side of the square and only some three
hundred yards away from Masson Hall. Much to her amusement, Henriette found that the conventions still had to

be respected; this was, after all, the era when Edinburgh professors still wore morning coats:[18]

> When I went to dinner at Professor Baldwin Brown's house, I had to go by carriage although his house was also in George Square. I hardly entered the carriage, when I had arrived! The same thing happened when the carriage called for me at 10 o'clock to bring me back to Masson Hall.

And she evidently appreciated his efforts to extend her social circle:

> I was invited to many houses, as Professor Baldwin Brown was anxious for me to meet different people. I also received many invitations as a result of the Professor making friends with a couple from the Fabian Society and was lucky enough to meet Bernard Shaw at dinner.

George Bernard Shaw, together with H. G. Wells, was one of the most prominent members of the Fabian Society, which had been founded in 1884 to promote the socialist cause. His presence in Edinburgh would no doubt have reflected the current revival of provincial Fabianism (which would reach a peak in 1913), and the recent re-establishment of the university's own Fabian Society.[19] It was clearly an extraordinarily different life for the unsophisticated seventeen-year-old girl who only the year before had left her Russian homeland for the first time, quite unable to speak a word of English.

Then, Henriette remembered, there were the evenings when 'sometimes we were rather naughty and left the Hall through a window, in order to go on the top of a bus in Princes Street. We also attended several dances given by the different students' clubs, and one of the wives of our Professors chaperoned us'.

But the Edinburgh climate proved too much for her. She became ill: 'I started to suffer from strong migraine, and the doctor thought that the fogs were bad for me and, at the end of the year, he said that I would not be able to stand another winter'. Meteorological Office reports do in fact suggest that the fog which pervaded the city throughout the winter of 1910–1911 was exceptionally persistent that year.[20] And when these thick fogs were intensified by smoke (not for nothing was Edinburgh colloquially known as Auld Reekie), this unhealthy combination often resulted in smog, a term recently coined by the ardent smoke abatement campaigner Dr Des Voeux.

Although Henriette had succeeded in passing the required examinations in Fine Art and Political Economy, her father reluctantly came to the conclusion that she would be unable to carry on with her studies. By the end of June 1911, Henriette would finally and with deep regret – 'it was a great blow to me' – have left Edinburgh for good. She did, however, take a great deal away with her: not only her newly acquired independence and adaptability but also the expectation that she could and should pursue a career. It was an experience that shaped her life. When Henriette returned to Libau she was accompanied by Leo Bennet, who 'stayed with us at the seaside for the whole summer'.

They continued to keep in touch:

I also used to hear from Miss Simson and Leo Bennet from Edinburgh. Miss Simson used to inform me of all the changes in Masson Hall and I had to write about my experiences. We kept up our correspondence till the outbreak of the war, and even at the beginning of the war letters came through to Russia.

Frances Simson retired in 1918. She lived in Edinburgh until her death in 1938, at the age of eighty-four. Masson Hall was demolished in the 1960s to make way for the new University Library. Ironically, the archival material relating to the university's first hall of residence for women is now housed in the modern building that replaced it.

Henriette grew up at a time when the pursuit of women's rights was rapidly gathering momentum. In October 1909, only days after her arrival in Edinburgh, large crowds had gathered to watch the great suffrage procession. It was by all accounts an impressive spectacle. Some 2,000 women suffragists had assembled at Bruntsfield Links, an open tract of land adjacent to the Meadows and only a short distance from Masson Hall. From there the long line of marchers, with their distinctive purple, white and green banners, had followed a route which led them directly through the centre of the city where crowds of spectators several rows deep lined both sides of Princes Street. A colourful procession that comprised a number of horse-drawn floats as well as a singular array of 'Historic characters' that included, *The Times* went on to report, such notable women as 'Mary Queen of Scots; the Duchess of Gordon...; the Countess of Buchan, who was imprisoned in an iron cage for crowning Bruce; Black Agnes, who defended Dunbar Castle for her husband; the Solway Firth martyrs, and Flora Macdonald'.[21]

As a resident of Masson Hall, Henriette would have been in a position to absorb the excitement of the occasion.

Indeed, her awareness of this public promotion of women's interests, together with her later experiences at the Hall, where the issue of women's suffrage was taken particularly seriously, would have made a strong impression on her. And there was, of course, Miss Simson's well-publicised support for the cause. The tone of Henriette's memoir reveals the profound admiration and respect she felt for this exceptional woman. 'Miss Simson', she wrote, 'was a wonderful person'; a role model and a source of inspiration for Henriette throughout the two highly formative years she spent in Edinburgh.

CHAPTER 6

FRANKFURT

Henriette was now free to pursue her musical ambitions. Her father, who, she explained, was keen that she should study in a milder climate, 'thought Frankfurt-am-Main was a suitable place. We went to Germany in 1912 and I was accepted at the Conservatoire for piano'.

Frankfurt was an excellent choice. The foundation of the Hoch Konservatorium (named after a generous local merchant) and the Frankfurt Musikschule in the second half of the nineteenth century[1] had established this cultured city as an important centre for musical education. In fact when the former had first opened in 1878 with the great Clara Schumann as the leading piano teacher, students had flocked to Frankfurt from far and wide.[2]

When Henriette herself was admitted to the Hoch Konservatorium in 1912 she was delighted when Alfred Hoehn, one of Germany's up-and-coming pianists, accepted her as a pupil – 'I was thinking of becoming a pianist', and Alfred Hoehn 'was one of the best professors'. The young professor had recently distinguished himself by winning the prestigious Rubinstein prize at the seventh international competition in St Petersburg.[3]

But this arrangement would be unexpectedly short-lived. The series of tests which Henriette had been obliged to undertake on first entering the school would reveal quite another aptitude, leading the Director of the Konservatorium to suggest that she 'should study singing and take piano as a second subject', an option that had never occurred to her before. 'A new life opened before me', she recalled. 'I always liked to sing and in school we had a good choir and there were a lot of lovely Russian folk-songs which we used to sing at home'.

Having only recently learnt that the Director, Iwan Knorr, had spent a good deal of time in Russia where he had been inspired by the rich tradition of Russian folk-song,[4] I could not help wondering whether it might perhaps have been Henriette's rendering of one of these Russian songs that had caused him to be, as she put it, so impressed by her 'natural singing voice'. If so, her choice may inadvertently have changed the course of her musical life.

When Professor Hoehn heard of this development he was not at all pleased and refused to take her on as a pupil. 'Professor Hoehn', Henriette acknowledged, 'said that as soon as one starts to devote one's time to singing, the piano takes second place and you cannot practise so many hours'. So although she carried on playing the piano, it was singing and the other related subjects that now became the principal focus of her studies: 'We had lessons in reading poetry, pronunciation and of course developing the vocal organs'. And there were classes on solfeggio and Dalcroze – 'the Dalcroze classes were very important. They were given by a well-known cellist who was himself a pupil of Dalcroze'. Named after the musical educator Emile Jaques-Dalcroze, this innovative system, combining music and movement, had originally been devised in the 1890s as a means of helping music students further their sense of rhythm.[5] Bearing in mind that Jaques-Dalcroze had actively begun to disseminate his system of Eurhythmics only a few years before Henriette entered the Konservatorium, these lessons would have constituted an unusual and innovative addition to the syllabus.

At the Hoch Konservatorium Henriette was taught to sing by a former 'pupil of Stockhausen'. A renowned Lieder singer, Julius Stockhausen had himself taught in Frankfurt for a time.[6] Lieder, the German word for art songs, have come to be associated with the works of poets such as Goethe and Schiller and with composers such as Schubert, Schumann, Brahms and Hugo Wolf. It was these German songs, these poems set to music, that would now become Henriette's great love as well as her inspiration. Indeed, as I write this in the twenty-first century, I can't help being conscious of how close my grandmother was to the Lied tradition of the nineteenth century.

But despite these credentials, Henriette was not entirely happy with her tuition. 'I must say', she admitted, 'I would have preferred to have my lessons with a woman singer. The difficulty was the breathing. In later years, I found that there is a difference to using your breath for a man and a woman'. All the same she was clearly making good progress and, even though she was one of the youngest students, she was 'chosen to sing in public' at the summer concert.

There was always a great deal of music to be heard in Frankfurt and Henriette took full advantage of her status as a student:

We really got a wonderful opportunity to hear the best music. Every two weeks we attended the rehearsals of the orchestras under the most famous conductors and

there was usually a fine soloist. We heard everybody
as Frankfurt, at that time, had a very high reputation
for music.

There was the irascible conductor Willem Mengelberg,
the principal conductor of Amsterdam's Concertgebouw
Orchestra. Mengelberg, whose behaviour at rehearsals was
legendary, also conducted Frankfurt's famous Museum
Concerts, of which he was the musical director between
1907 and 1920.[7] Although, as Henriette recollected:

> He only used to come for a few rehearsals before the
> concerts. The critics were very annoyed about it and
> were not at all favourable towards him. There was a
> great quarrel and Mengelberg prohibited the critics
> from attending his concerts, which was a great pity
> for the soloists and musicians.

The prolonged and acrimonious dispute that preceded
this embargo had undoubtedly created quite a stir: 'The
city is musically in a state of war', reported *The Musical
Times*, 'owing to the severe criticisms that the *Frankfurter
Zeitung* has been passing upon the conductor of the
Museumsgesellschaft Concerts', with the subscribers even
going so far as to demonstrate 'against the newspaper'.[8]

> But, of course, there were other guest conductors. We
> heard Rachmaninoff, Medtner and Schnabel and all
> the vocal celebrities. We also had to attend the opera
> and I heard the Ring by Wagner several times. We
> were encouraged to hear as much as possible and we
> learned to appreciate good music.

At the beginning of June, there was a memorable Brahms Festival in nearby Wiesbaden. The comprehensive programme included all four of Brahms's Symphonies[9] and 'they [also]', Henriette added, 'performed the *Neue Liebeslieder* for four voices, accompanied by two pianists and one of the pianists was Schnabel. It was an unforgettable four days'. And the chance to hear a number of notable artists, from the distinguished pianist Arthur Schnabel to the virtuoso violinist Fritz Kreisler, to whom Sir Edward Elgar had recently dedicated his acclaimed Violin Concerto in B Minor.[10]

It was always difficult to get student accommodation in the city and Henriette initially had to make do with a room on the top floor of a pension. Three other students from the music school also had rooms in this top floor eyrie and it was excessively noisy: 'We all practised nearly at the same time and it was impossible to hear oneself. There was a violinist, a piano pupil and another singer'. When Henriette's parents came to see her a few months later, her mother was shocked 'as she could not imagine [how] I could work with the dreadful noise. My parents found another pension for me but I did feel lonely without my three musicians'.

Not long afterwards, one of these musicians would become the recipient of my great-grandfather's extraordinary generosity:

> I remember my fellow singer at the pension was a charming girl and we became great friends. One day she got a wire that her father had died. He was a professor in one of the small universities. There were no funds left for her to continue her stay at the

Conservatoire. I spoke to my father on the telephone and told him about it. He told me to make immediate arrangements with the bank to pay her usual monthly allowance that she used to get and *no names to be mentioned*. She was the happiest person in the world and said that she was full of gratitude to whoever was looking after her.

During the Easter holidays, Henriette's parents took her 'to Italy, to Rome and other cities'. Her father was indefatigable, 'determined that we should see everything, which was tiring, as we had to get up at 6 o'clock'. After Italy, they moved on to the South of France, to Menton 'where we rode donkeys in the mountains'. Popular with nineteenth-century tourists, these excursions had evidently lost none of their allure. Following the old mule-drivers' paths, riding their donkeys along the steeply winding tracks, they visited some of the 'smaller places near Menton', mountain villages such as Castellar or perhaps Sainte-Agnes perched high above the town. Then, after spending a few days in Nice – 'At last we had a little rest at Nice' – they went to Monte Carlo where, much to Henriette's disappointment, she 'was not permitted to enter the casino'; admittance to the legendary gaming rooms was restricted to those over twenty-one years of age.

The Côte d'Azur, once the preserve of the English aristocracy, had long appealed to Russian visitors. From the late 1850s onwards, members of the imperial family, together with a number of their compatriots, had made their way to the Riviera. And wealthy Russians had carried on undertaking the journey, generally arriving in some style.[11] Russian artists had also gravitated there: in February 1899, the

French première of Glinka's *A Life for the Tsar* was staged before a glittering audience at the Opera House in Nice[12]; the great Russian singer Feodor Chaliapin would appear at Garnier's sumptuous Théâtre de Monte-Carlo.[13] And in 1911, only the year before Henriette's visit, Sergei Diaghilev had brought his Ballets Russes dancers to the principality.[14]

So it was perhaps not surprising that Henriette's father had chosen to explore this part of the world. And perhaps significant too that the charm, not to mention the cachet, of a holiday on the French Riviera should have made such an impression on his elder daughter; the Côte d'Azur was, after all, the most fashionable winter destination in Europe. While the mild climate had once constituted the principal attraction, the social calendar was now punctuated by operas and ballets, horse races and regattas[15] and such spectacular events as the *'meeting d'aviation'*, the air show that had marked the end of the high season in Nice in April 1910.

Henriette duly returned to Frankfurt. But, sadly, the following year, her days as a student all too soon came to an end:

> At the beginning of April [1913] I got a telegram from my father that my mother was very ill at a hospital in Königsberg [now Kaliningrad]. I packed my things and left to be with my mother. We brought her back to Riga, where they now lived, and [I] never went back to Frankfurt...

Always devoted to her mother, Henriette had clearly felt compelled to put her duty as a daughter before her musical ambitions. There would, however, be other occasions when the music would come first.

CHAPTER 7

RIGA

Riga 1913: a city of parks and gardens, of nineteenth-century boulevards flanked by handsome buildings, of theatrically innovative Art Nouveau confections. This engaging and highly commercial metropolis, with just over half a million inhabitants, was one of imperial Russia's largest cities, arguably the most important export centre in the Empire. The key to her prosperity lay on the banks of the river, in the winding streets of the Old Town, in the sheltered natural harbour and in the busy port area.

In 1913, the Inner Town or Old Town, which had once been contained within defensive ramparts, was a maze of narrow streets, old buildings and soaring spires. The cathedral, the churches, the castle, the houses of the Great and Small Guilds all jostled for attention in an area so small that it could be crossed on foot in under a quarter of an hour. On the banks of the river, the busy quays and warehouses dealt with the exports and imports that ensured the city's wealth and prosperity.

There was the fourteenth-century House of the Blackheads, at one time a venue for foreign merchants, and one of the oldest buildings in the city. The ornate façade, extensively embellished over the years, displayed a riotous jumble of Renaissance-inspired ornament amongst which the arms of Riga, Hamburg, Lübeck and Bremen stood out – a clear visual reminder that Riga had been a Hansa Town, one of the earliest members of the Hanseatic League[1] – the powerful trading organisation that once dominated the Baltic and the North Sea.[2]

Beside the Old Town, Riga Castle, constantly rebuilt and extended over the years, looked back not only to the age of the Teutonic Knights but also to the seventeenth century when the town had for a time come under Swedish rule. Yet another chapter in Riga's history was illustrated by the extensively restored Powder Tower, sole survivor of the fortifications that had formerly surrounded the town.

But the Inner Town was no fossilised museum of history; when the Great Guild had been reconstructed in the middle of the nineteenth century, a new Stock Exchange had been erected at the same time. In 1913, the Old Town was still the city's commercial district and the solid nineteenth- and early twentieth-century edifices that crowded the narrow streets housed many of Riga's leading banks and businesses.

It was here that Henriette's father had established his main office. Over the previous decade he had been both fortunate enough and astute enough to take full advantage of the meteoric expansion of the Russian wood industry; an industry which, the *Russian Year-Book for 1911* confirms, had seen the quantity of exports grow by fifty-four per cent between 1901 and 1907.[3] By 1913, my great-grandfather had risen to become one of Riga's leading exporters of wood and his company was one of the most successful firms in the city. In keeping with this prosperity, he was registered as a merchant of the first guild, the highest rank in a trading hierarchy that was largely dependent on wealth.[4]

At his timber yard on the banks of the Düna (the Western Dvina, now the Daugava) River, he would have processed some of the vast quantities of logs that reached the city in the spring, once the water levels had risen after the thaw.[5] So numerous were these great rafts of logs that by 1914 Riga was reputed to be 'the most important timber port of the world'.[6] A Latvian publication of the 1920s (*Latvia as a transit country*) vividly conjures up this area of timber yards and saw-mills:

> The upper and more shallow part of the [Riga] harbour is an extensive and natural timber harbour, where there is room for up to 15,000 rafts of timber at once. On the banks there are a number of saw-mills, for sawing wood to prepare it for its further transport to Western Europe. The timber harbour offers a curious picture, when for a distance of 10 kilometres every side-stream and also the main channel of the river is completely covered with rafts, only a narrow strip of water being seen, which is necessarily kept open for the passage of a whole fleet of tugs, barges and ferry-boats.[7]

But there was another side to Riga: after the old ramparts had been demolished in the middle of the nineteenth century, the town had quickly expanded; the Inner Town was soon surrounded by a ring of boulevards and the former defensive moat was transformed into a canal and set amidst landscaped gardens. With the creation of parks and boulevards and new residential districts, Riga acquired an unprecedented aura of sophistication.

Had Henriette patronised the café on the Bastion Hill (Bastejkalns) that first summer, she would have been in a position to enjoy some of the best views of the boulevards.

From this raised vantage point, she could have looked out over the canal gardens towards Theatre Boulevard (Aspazijas bulvāris), Alexander Boulevard (Brīvības iela) and Nikolai Boulevard (K.Valdemāra iela), to name but a few of the streets that criss-crossed the city centre. Planted with linden trees, these wide avenues were lined with solid and imposing apartment buildings, some gothic, some classical, others Italianate in style, all suggesting a certain bourgeois security.

It is fortunate that, even after two world wars and almost half a century of Soviet occupation, the layout of this part of the city appears to be more or less as it was in 1913: the canal gardens still form the nucleus of the city centre and tree-lined boulevards continue to surround the Old Town with its narrow streets. Many buildings have survived, while others have been restored or otherwise reconstructed.

And Riga still has her parks and gardens, gardens that would have been very much at the heart of life in Riga. The canal gardens, a well-planned municipal space with clearly marked paths, well-tended flowerbeds and carefully grouped clusters of trees, were traversed daily by many of the town's residents. In nearby Wöhrmann Park (Vērmanes dārzs), which featured 'a *Mineral Water Establishment*' as well as 'a fair *Restaurant*',[8] summer evenings were enlivened by the military band, which played until eleven at night. Next to Wöhrmann Park, the Esplanade Gardens, overlooked by Riga's great Orthodox Cathedral, constituted yet another public space. To the north, the Kaiserlicher Garden (Viestura dārzs) was a popular venue for 'concerts and variety performances in summer, skating and tobogganing in winter'.[9]

Then there were the theatres: the City Theatre (now the Latvian National Opera), a fine building with a monumental classical façade, where performances were given in German; the Russian Theatre, an impressive early twentieth-century edifice; and the Latvian Theatre. They not only exemplified Riga's multiplicity of languages but also conveniently reflected the character and shifting social composition of the city itself. Despite her incorporation into the Russian Empire at the beginning of the eighteenth century, the Baltic port of Riga had retained her cultural affinity with Germany; it was not until the second half of the nineteenth century that tsarist Russification measures, coupled with the rise of Latvian nationalism, would to a certain extent succeed in altering the status quo.[10]

Riga's early twentieth-century prosperity had coincided with a number of exciting architectural developments. In Elisabethstrasse (Elizabetes iela), named after Peter the Great's daughter the Russian Empress Elizaveta Petrovna, and the surrounding streets, innovative structures rose almost daily. Among the most striking were the flamboyant Art Nouveau edifices conceived by Mikhail Eisenstein, father of the film director Sergei Eisenstein. Their façades embellished with arresting sculptural motifs – elaborate figures, giant faces, sphinxes – these buildings, together with those designed by the many other architects who worked so creatively in Riga in the early years of the twentieth century, would have made this a fascinating and invigorating place to live.

There was a huge demand for modern buildings equipped with lifts, up-to-date plumbing and central heating.[11] And indeed in the years immediately preceding the war over a thousand new business and apartment buildings would be erected each year.[12] With gas-lit streets, electric trams and improved sewage and water systems,[13] Riga was by now a truly modern city.

Henriette would have spent much of the summer of 1913 at the Rigascher Strand, the easily accessible coastal area where her father had recently acquired a villa. The opening of a new railway line in the 1870s had swiftly transformed what had once been a number of small fishing villages on the shores of the Gulf of Riga into a series of summer resorts: Bilderlingshof, Edinburg, Majorenhof, Dubbeln, Karlsbad, Assern. Conveniently located, within easy commuting distance from Riga, these villages (I have used the more customary German rather than the Russian names[14]) were not only bathing resorts but also places where whole families could stay for the entire season.

Each resort had its own distinctive character: whereas Dubbeln (Dubulti) was the oldest and Majorenhof (Majori) the busiest, Edinburg (named after the Grand Duchess Maria Alexandrovna, the daughter of the Russian Tsar Alexander II, who had married Queen Victoria's second son Prince Alfred, Duke of Edinburgh), with its fine villas, was considered to be the grandest and most aristocratic.

The villages of the Rigascher Strand (present-day Jurmala) were confined to a long narrow strip of land with the sea on one side and the meandering Courland Aa (the Lielupe) on the other. Each resort had its own railway station as well as a number of public buildings such as hotels and Kurhäuser – these "cure houses" not only offered treatments but also generally provided other amenities such as restaurants and casinos. At Bilderlingshof (Bulduri), a contemporary view of the Kurhaus reveals a spacious court-yard filled with numerous tables and folding metal chairs. The embellished white tablecloths, the waiters standing to attention, indicate that this was a smart and no doubt well-patronised outdoor restaurant. Another view, this time of

Edinburg (Dzintari), shows an arched gateway surrounded by tall pine trees; a prominently-lettered sign confirms that this is the entrance to the combined Kasino-Kurhaus.

Fashionable Edinburg, which had the distinction of having two stations, boasted a casino, restaurants and concert-gardens. The large Kurhaus had its own sea-pavilion, an unusual Art Nouveau structure of iron and glass. Next door, on the dunes, Dr Maximovitch's Sanatorium offered a variety of treatments such as medicinal baths. Both the Kurhaus and the impressive timber-built Sanatorium, which had been erected in 1906, were unusual in that they were among the few permanent public buildings that had direct access to the beach.

At nearby Majorenhof, too, 'the most crowded and popular of the resorts on the Riga coast',[15] there was a concert-garden and a splendid turreted sea-pavilion, with a substantial tree-filled terrace, which led directly on to the sands. In summer, when the jovial sound of music filled the air, one contemporary traveller noted the swarms of visitors thronging the streets and parks while military bands played a stirring medley of German and Russian tunes.[16]

Sea-bathing was inevitably one of the Riga Strand's principal attractions, and in the interests of propriety all the resorts enforced the same strictly regulated hours, with men and women bathing at separate times. In the summer of 1913, Henriette would have found that she was only permitted to bathe between 10 and 1 in the morning and between 3 and 5.30 in the afternoon,[17] with men taking their sea-baths in the early morning and the early afternoon. Extensive bathing jetties, topped with wooden huts or cabins, would also have done much to protect the bathers' modesty. These temporary structures, which were renewed every year, extended into the shallow sea as far as the third offshore sandbar.[18]

Walking, another beneficial form of exercise, was a popular pastime. Residents and visitors alike could stroll in the public parks or follow the many footpaths through the woods or promenade across the firm sands. And, at Bilderlingshof, they could enjoy the magnificent views from the seaside park which had been laid out on the dunes.

With few private houses directly overlooking the beach, all the summer cottages and villas nestled on plots of land set among the tall pine trees. But although the majority of these late nineteenth- and early twentieth-century houses were of timber construction, they were not of uniform appearance. Towers, gables and elaborately carved wooden details adorned some of the more distinguished of these dwelling houses. Displaying an eclectic variety of architectural styles, which would have greatly contributed to the charm of the district, they would no doubt have reminded Henriette of Libau.

It was an area she would always love – 'I think it was the most beautiful place that I have ever seen'. Years later, when she wistfully remembered the 'wonderful beach with golden sand, which stretched for miles with pine woods on the top', she would recall the distinctive smell of the pine trees with a nostalgic longing. Henriette relished the outdoor life: searching for mushrooms in the forests; following the wooden pathways across the dunes and descending the steps on to the beach; walking for miles along the seemingly endless sands; or bathing in the cold but invigorating sea. It was the last summer before the war and she was still only nineteen years old.

CHAPTER 8

ST PETERSBURG

At the end of the summer, Henriette returned to Riga where she met and subsequently 'got married to a young lawyer. He just came from St Petersburg for a holiday', she wrote, 'fell in love with the city and made it his home. He was quite well known as for his first case he had to defend a soldier who was court-martialled…My future husband had worked hard at the case, persuaded the jury of the soldier's innocence, and got him free. There was enormous publicity and he became a very busy lawyer'.

It had been love at first sight. Their first meeting, which I believe took place at the opera, was, for my grandmother, the beginning of a life-long romance. But Henriette was only twenty, some ten years younger than Osip, her future husband, and it may well have been this age discrepancy which led her parents to forbid the marriage. Undeterred and deeply in love, no longer the obedient girl she had been at sixteen, she decided to elope and, by claiming that she was already twenty-one years old, she succeeded in dispensing with her parents' consent.

A few months later, Henriette and Osip took a brief holiday, or maybe even a belated honeymoon: 'We managed to go over to Finland for a few days and enjoyed the beautiful country just before war was declared. I shall never forget the fast horses who took us over the place and the small islands going by boat round the coast'.

Today, many of the rocky, tree-clad islands near to Helsingfors (Helsinki) still appear to be relatively unspoilt, with here and there a tantalising glimpse of an attractive wooden house dating from the early years of the twentieth century. From Helsingfors, Henriette and Osip may well have taken a twenty-minute steamer ride to Sveaborg (Suomenlinna), the Russian naval fortress (now a picturesque but nonetheless impressive ruin) which once guarded the entrance to the southern harbour. Or perhaps they ventured somewhat further afield among the 'Finnish Skerries',[1] the beautiful islands much loved by Tsar Nicholas II.

They went on to spend a few days in St Petersburg. Fortunately for Henriette, their visit coincided with the time of the 'White Nights' so that, for her, the beauty of the city would be for ever associated with those long light nights when the sun never seemed to set.

From the gilded dome of St Isaac's Cathedral to the multi-coloured façade of the Church of the Resurrection, from the sheer grandeur of the imperial Winter Palace to the more intimate scale of the smaller private palaces, Henriette was entranced. Osip knew St Petersburg well and I should like to think that he took his new wife to Vasilievsky Island to see the former Building of the Twelve Colleges, the Baroque edifice that housed the university where he had once been a student in the Faculty of Jurisprudence.

Only the previous year, St Petersburg had ceremoniously commemorated the tercentenary of the founding of the Romanov dynasty. In February 1913 thousands of guests[2] had come, many of them from the farthest corners of the Empire, to attend a service of thanksgiving in the Kazan Cathedral. To look at photographs taken that day of the imperial family (the Tsar with the eight-year-old Tsarevich,

the Dowager-Empress and the Tsarina, their daughters
the four Grand Duchesses) driving in their carriages from
the Winter Palace to the Nevsky Prospekt,[3] one could be
forgiven for assuming that all was well with the Russian
Empire. St Petersburg was *en fête*: the principal streets were
bedecked with flags[4] and decorated with portraits of the
tsars,[5] and several of the city's most historic monuments
were illuminated.[6]

But in reality the Tsar rarely visited his capital. 'Ever since
the revolutionary outbreak that had followed the Japanese
War', the British Ambassador Sir George Buchanan
confirmed, 'the Emperor and Empress had lived in compara-
tive retirement at Tsarskoe Selo...'[7] The problems that had
surfaced in 1905 still rankled; the Tsar's autocratic rule and
his attitude towards the Duma continued to exacerbate the
tensions within the state.[8] With the revival of the trade
union movement, workers were becoming more militant:[9]
over the coming year the number of industrial strikes would
significantly increase.[10]

Henriette and Osip would no doubt have stayed at one of
the city's leading hotels: the recently opened Astoria, billed
as the most modern hotel in Russia, advertised telephone
and up-to-date plumbing in each one of its 350 rooms as
well as a central vacuum cleaning system and electric venti-
lation; the totally remodelled and refurbished Grand Hotel
d'Europe was justifiably proud of its large roof garden, with
its shady pergolas and magnificent views.[11]

All the finest establishments were not only within a
few minutes' walk of the Nevsky Prospekt, St Petersburg's
great thoroughfare, but also of 'the Morskaia' which, in
the opinion of one contemporary English writer, was 'the
only street where trade assumes a certain splendour'.[12] And

indeed it was here that Henriette would have found the shop of the famous goldsmith and jeweller Peter Carl Fabergé.

Of the six top goldsmiths and jewellers[13] who had their premises in this exclusive street, Fabergé was the most well known. For the past thirty years the family firm had been responsible for producing the magnificent imperial Easter eggs. Privately commissioned, these exquisitely decorated, highly ornate eggs each contained a 'surprise', whether portraits of the imperial children, a model of the Tsar's yacht (the Standardt), or the miniature gold train, elaborated in about 1900, which had been skilfully concealed in an egg engraved with a map of the Trans-Siberian Railway. While these confections had invariably been confined to the imperial family, smaller and less expensive eggs could be bought in the shop, which also sold other items such as cigar lighters, cigarette cases and small picture frames.[14]

Fabergé had opened their new premises at 24 Morskaya Street in 1900. The impressive four-storey building housed the firm's studios and workshops as well as the family's living quarters and the famous salesroom.[15] As befitted the commercial nature of the premises, the tallest windows were on the ground floor and the bulbous red granite columns which divided the high plate-glass windows provided a strong visual contrast to the stone and grey granite of the upper floors.[16]

Standing outside the former Fabergé headquarters only a few years ago, I was struck by how imposing and monumental the entrance and showroom level of the building must have been. And yet, at the same time, how discreet: the clear and simple FABERGÉ inscription either side of the main door (Latin lettering on one side, Cyrillic the other[17]) the only indication as to the nature of what lay within.

An old black-and-white photograph of the interior of the ground floor salesroom confirms that here too a certain austerity was considered appropriate, from the plain wall cabinets with their mirror-fronted doors,[18] to the waist-high wooden display counters, the central chandelier and the low-hanging pendant lights. It was the Fabergé artefacts in their open boxes, tantalisingly visible beneath the glass tops of the counters, that were, fittingly, at the heart of the room.

In the Fabergé showroom, Henriette bought a wedding present for her husband: a plain gold cigarette case made in the company's workshops. A gift which, ironically, would all too soon come to acquire an even more poignant significance; my grandfather's cigarette case would not only come to be a lasting reminder of their visit but also of pre-war, pre-revolution, tsarist St Petersburg. The Fabergé firm, one of the casualties of the revolution, was nationalised in 1918. The staff were dismissed, the stock was sold and Peter Carl Fabergé himself fled from Russia. He would die in exile in Lausanne in 1920.[19]

Despite the beauty of the city and the radiance of the 'White Nights', this was 1914 and the shadow of war was looming. In August, in response to anti-German sentiment, St Petersburg was renamed Petrograd.[20] Ten years later, shortly after Lenin's death, Petrograd had become Leningrad.

CHAPTER 9

WAR

In the spring of 1914 Henriette and Osip would have found that the political situation in St Petersburg was becoming increasingly volatile. When the French President paid an official visit to the city in July, the growing discontent would result in a general strike:[1] trams were brought to a halt, trains ceased to run and, as the strikes spread, rioters took to the streets.[2]

The strikers, *The Times* reported, had 'felled…telegraph poles…with saws and axes, and constructed barricades with the poles and paving stones. Wires were stretched across the street and stones were scattered about everywhere in order to impede the Cossacks' horses'. The newspaper's correspondent described how the Cossacks, presumably undeterred by these obstructions, had 'dismounted and advanced with rifles', only to be assaulted by 'revolver shots and stones. They replied by firing, and the strikers fled, carrying off their wounded'.[3]

The French President had set out from France in the middle of July (beginning of July OS) with the intention of undertaking a round of state visits. Russia, France's ally, was to be his first port of call, followed by Sweden, Denmark and Norway. The international situation did not as yet preclude foreign travel: the German Kaiser was still pursuing his summer holiday in the Norwegian fjords[4] and, only a day or so before President Poincaré's departure, the Tsar and his family had embarked on a 'yachting cruise in the Finnish Skerries'.[5]

It was a hot summer. In England, where the mercury had occasionally topped ninety degrees Fahrenheit,[6] the weather was evidently taking its toll: 'We have had enough heat this summer', complained *The Times*, confidently asserting that 'almost anything now begins to seem better than the London streets'.[7] On Monday 20 July 1914, the day that the French President was due to arrive in Russia, the newspaper's readers were presented with 'SUGGESTIONS FOR THE HOLIDAYS'. Billed as 'INCREASING TEMPTATIONS TO TRAVEL', 'TRIPS AT HOME AND ABROAD',[8] the article purported to pick out some of the most enticing routes on offer:

> St Petersburg *via* the Kiel Canal suggests the United Shipping Company…, and tempts us with views of the chief sights of St Petersburg and Moscow. The same agency sets forth the advantages of the Harwich-Esjberg route by the steamers of the Forenedo Line of Copenhagen, for trips to Copenhagen and Libau.[9]

As the writer remarked, 'the attractions of Northern Europe alone seem enough to absorb the whole holiday population of the British Isles'.[10]

On the evening of 23 July (10 July OS) President Poincaré concluded his visit to Russia by entertaining the Tsar, together with the imperial family, to a farewell banquet on board the French battleship *France*.[11] Shortly afterwards, the French President set sail for Stockholm. But within days the international situation had deteriorated to such an extent that he would be obliged to curtail his visit to Scandinavia and return to Paris.[12]

Events moved swiftly. On 28 July (15 July OS), Austria declared war on Serbia. On 1 August (19 July OS), Germany declared war on Russia. The following day, Sunday 2 August (20 July OS), Nicholas II reciprocated by declaring war on Germany. On 3 August (21 July OS), a German warship, the *Augsburg*, opened fire on the naval base at Libau.[13] And just one day later, on Tuesday 4 August 1914, Great Britain declared war on Germany.

While the British public had endured a dispiriting August Bank Holiday weekend, some 300 miles to the west of St Petersburg, Henriette had been taking a holiday at the Rigascher Strand:

> We were spending the summer at the seaside near Riga...It was not a long summer as in the middle of July [OS] war was declared and we all moved back to town. One was not sure where the first assault was going to happen. The trains were crowded with soldiers, coming from all over Russia.

She witnessed their initial enthusiasm – 'we saw trains passing with soldiers singing along', trains which would have been conveying Russian troops to the west. But their cheerfulness would be short-lived: of the two Russian armies that were sent into East Prussia, one would be crushingly defeated at the battle of Tannenberg; the other would be repulsed by the German army at the battle of the Masurian Lakes. By the end of August (OS), these soldiers would have been forced to retreat across the border, to seek refuge on Russian soil.[14]

Although the aftermath of this tragic rout brought a lull in the fighting, the onset of war had forced Henriette to assess her own situation. 'One had to make plans', she wrote, 'to leave the vulnerable city. It was a difficult decision. I was expecting a baby and was not very strong'. In the event, the letup in the fighting and the prolonged stalemate[15] would allow her to remain in Riga for the birth of her child. Henriette was twenty-one years old when, at the end of December 1914, her daughter Tatiana (my mother) was born.

The following year brought a new set of problems. In the spring of 1915, the Germans invaded Courland. Shortly afterwards they captured Libau. Henriette would later complain that her home town had effectively been abandoned, a view which would no doubt have reflected popular opinion:

> Libau was the easiest target, as Kaiser Wilhelm persuaded the Russian Czar Nikolai to close the fortress in Libau, as he said 'there will never be a war between us'. And so the German army entered Libau without any battle and they stayed there until the end of the war.

The Russians had very few troops in Courland and the Germans entered virtually unopposed, Stanley Washburn, the *Times* special correspondent with the Russian Armies, confirmed in 1915.[16] And the newspaper's correspondent in Petrograd, reinforcing the perception that the town no longer held any importance, reported that Libau had for some time ceased operating as a naval fortress.[17]

By the beginning of July, Riga was under threat. The German army was advancing eastwards: Windau (Ventspils), the ice-free harbour some 70 miles up the coast from Libau, was taken on 5 July (OS); on the 19th (OS), Mitau (Jelgava), 15 miles southwest of Riga, succumbed.[18] Hundreds of thousands of refugees fled from Courland alone as up to two-thirds of the population evaded the German occupation.[19]

When it became increasingly apparent that Riga might fall, factories, '[g]overnment institutions and other establishments'[20] were evacuated and inhabitants and workers alike joined the relentless tide of refugees. While arrangements had been put in place for the relocation of important concerns,[21] others were left to organise their own means of escape. 'The evacuation from Riga is in full swing', the *Times* correspondent in Petrograd reported on 23 July (OS), 'the streets are packed with dense crowds, and the stations are besieged with those anxious to depart'.[22]

Henriette too had begun to fear the worst: 'We were advised to leave Riga, as it was very vulnerable and one knew that the Germans would like to take it as soon as possible'. With the means and the incentive to organise their departure, they set out with a 'wagon' crammed with their possessions, including Henriette's precious Steinway.

However, despite numerous offensives, another two years would elapse before the German army finally succeeded in capturing the city.

CHAPTER 10

AN ESTATE IN THE COUNTRY

The summer of 1915 became a summer of retreat as, from July (OS) onwards,[1] not only the Russian army but also countless civilians were forced to flee. In their search for a safe haven, these displaced people inevitably moved into the Russian interior.[2]

Henriette was fortunate in that she had somewhere to go. Over the years her father had acquired several large estates in Russia and he 'decided on the one nearer to Moscow. It was very convenient, as that particular estate was near a railway station'. She would later describe this 'enormous wood estate' as 'a marvellous place', so large that it 'took twelve hours on horseback to go' round the whole property. 'My father was quite an extraordinary man. He was a fanatic about woods'.

Henriette's enthusiasm and subsequent nostalgia for this richly forested area made it clear that she had both understood and recognised her father's passion. 'My father', Henriette observed, was also 'a great specialist [on woods] and supervised a lot of the work in the winter' —the best time for cutting timber. A benevolent employer:

> He was a wonderful man, looking after the peasants who worked for him and there also used to come hundreds of other workmen to cut the woods. A special

house was built for the workmen with facilities of a Russian bath [*banya*]. There was also a shop for them, subsidised by my father, so that they could buy everything very cheaply.

It was interesting to hear him talk about the care he took for his workmen. If there were any complaints he personally arranged to see them. The same went for the peasants near the estate. They could use the shop and also could get all the wood for their personal use. It was a very nice atmosphere and they all adored my father and called him little father [*batyushka*]. Later on we will see that the Russian peasants never forgot what he did for them.

The area around Nelidovo abounded with lakes and streams, many of which, in turn, flowed into the Western Dvina. And it was along this river and its tributaries that he would have arranged for his logs to be floated to Riga in the spring, once the water levels had risen after the snow and ice had thawed. This was the most convenient as well as the cheapest form of transport. Where the river was large enough the logs were made into rafts, where it was not the logs floated downriver accompanied by workmen whose job it was to stop the wood from getting trapped on the riverbanks.[3] Once these logs, too, could be fastened together they would journey along the Western Dvina to meet up with the numerous other rafts congregating in Riga's upper harbour.

In the early years of the twentieth century, Riga was Russia's largest timber-exporting port, handling more volume than either St Petersburg-Cronstadt or Archangel.[4]

And with timber yards and sawmills, both at Riga and at Libau, dealing with great quantities of fir and pine from Russia's northwest, my great-grandfather would have been in an enviable position and his business would have been immensely profitable. Personally responsible for the entire production chain of what must have been a considerable operation, his wide-ranging involvement in all aspects of the enterprise, from the forestry, to the sawmills, to the export side of the company, would have been crucial for the success of the business. Henriette's account suggests that her father was sending wood to Germany as well as to Great Britain, which was the leading export market for Russian timber.

Nevertheless, while she was quite happy to spend the summer of 1915 on her father's estate, Henriette clearly had no intention of staying on there for the winter: 'My sister had to go to school and', she admitted, 'I was longing to go to Moscow and continue my music'. As the estate was only:

> about six hours by train from Moscow, it was easy to reach. Later on my father made arrangements for the train to stop for a moment, if we were on the train from Moscow, and let us down, so that we did not have to go by horses from the station. They put on some steps and it was very convenient.

To secure this concession Henriette's father would have had to negotiate with the Moscow-Vindava-Rybinsk Railway, the private company that operated the line which ran from Moscow to Riga and then on to Vindava (Windau).[5] Many years later, in his epic novel *August 1914*, the writer

Alexander Solzhenitsyn would devise a similar arrangement for the fictitious Tomchak family who, in order to alight from the express train, had paid several hundred roubles for such a permit.[6]

CHAPTER 11

MOSCOW

When she first set out for Moscow in the autumn of 1915, Henriette had initially only intended to look for 'some rooms' in the city; Osip was in the army and she had decided that she 'could safely leave Tatiana with a nanny and my mother in the country'. She soon changed her mind. 'The most urgent problem', she recalled, 'was to find a house, as I wanted my child with us. At that time Moscow was already very overcrowded, as many people wanted to be away from the war, and it was difficult to get somewhere'.

Henriette knew that she would have to be resourceful:

I went on a walking tour through all the small streets to see if I could find something suitable. People did not advertise at that time, as they were afraid to get the wrong people. After a few days I was at last to see a house just finished by workmen. After I had a talk with them, they explained to me that the house was built for the Director of the Moscow Conservatoire, Ippolitov-Ivanov. It was at the Arbat, in the middle of the city and was quite unusual. Now that it was ready, he did not like it, as the windows were rather high. I did not waste any time, got in touch with the owner, and we bought it. It even had a little garden at the back of the house – which of course was perfect. It was an ideal place for the family to live in...

When I came to visit Moscow almost a hundred years later, I began to consider where this building might have been located. Acting on the assumption that for the sake of convenience the distinguished Russian composer and conductor, Mikhail Ippolitov-Ivanov, might well have chosen a site near to the music school for his prospective residence, I decided to focus on the network of streets that lay between the old Arbat Square and the Conservatoire on Bolshaya Nikitskaya Street.

Having ascertained that the Conservatoire was in fact only a ten-minute walk away, I proceeded to explore many of the smaller streets and cobbled lanes (the *pereulok*) in the vicinity of Arbat Square itself. Deeply conscious that this was the part of the city where Henriette and Tatiana might have lived, I was delighted to find that despite the construction, the destruction, the innovation and the renovation that had taken place throughout the course of the intervening century, something still remained of the rural ambience[1] that had once characterised this corner of Moscow.

Henriette has described the house as being 'in a good part of Moscow', and indeed the Arbatskaya was considered to be one of Moscow's most exclusive districts.[2] But there was another side to the Arbat, one which I believe would also have appealed to her. It was an area redolent with historical and literary associations: the Arbat had at times been home to some of Russia's greatest literary figures, from Alexander Pushkin and Mikhail Lermontov in the nineteenth century to Andrei Bely and the Nobel Prize-winning author Ivan Bunin in the early years of the twentieth.

The Arbat's unique character was to some extent due to the way in which the district had evolved. Formerly inhabited by the nobility, by the end of the nineteenth century the

Arbat had become popular with the up-and-coming cultural elite who would soon be joined by Moscow's professional classes, keen to experience life in this desirable neighbourhood. When Henriette came to walk along Arbat Street in 1915, she would have come across a delightful mixture of buildings, ranging from the low one- or two-storey neoclassical houses, which dated from the first half of the nineteenth century, to the new apartment buildings, which had been erected around the beginning of the twentieth.[3] The latter, with their modern conveniences, also served as a showcase for the latest architectural styles.

But the charm of the Arbat would have been most apparent in the 'small streets', where most of the houses would have had gardens. While I can only imagine what the family house might have looked like, Henriette's memoir does provide a number of helpful clues: it was a 'big house', it was 'on one floor' and it had 'strange high windows'. Bearing in mind that there was a neo-classical revival in Moscow at the time,[4] it is probably safe to assume that Ippolitov-Ivanov's architect would have been looking back to the substantial one- or two-storey residences of the early to mid-nineteenth century. Many of these houses would have displayed an unbroken façade punctuated by unusually tall windows, which were generally substantially raised from the ground.

Henriette recollected that:

It [the house] could accommodate the whole family. We had to make arrangements for my sister, who was twelve years old, to get into a school, and my brother to the university. We had brought a wagon from Riga with our furniture and my Steinway and life seemed to be quite normal, so far away from the war. I could practise many hours a day as I had the old nanny from Riga (who was by now in her seventies) and she was very reliable.

I had decided not to enter the Conservatoire, but have private lessons for singing and piano. It was difficult to find a proper singing professor. I went to all the concerts to see what I could learn. One evening I heard the singer Anna El-Tour and was enchanted and I knew that she was the person who could give me all the knowledge.

Only a few years older than Henriette, Anna El-Tour had already made a name for herself both at home and abroad. On the occasion of her London début in 1908 the *Times* reviewer had fulsomely praised '…the full volume of her fine soprano voice…as well as her power of giving emotional intensity to the climax of the song'.[5] Some eight years later this accomplished singer had also become a sought-after teacher and it took a great deal of persuasion on Henriette's part before El-Tour would agree to accept her as a student:

She did take me on, although she took only a few pupils, and I had some wonderful two and a half years of her guidance and help. She was also a marvellous pianist and could accompany everything. And now I could really devote my time to my studies and prepare a programme for my future. Anna El-Tour was the ideal person, as she herself had worked very hard, before she became the well-known concert singer. She spoke several languages fluently and we could go through a good deal of songs in French, English and Russian of course.

But there was evidently more to life in Moscow than music. Russian cultural historian Rosamund Bartlett has described how during the reign of Nicholas II 'an explosion of creative talent took place across all the arts'.[6] This was Moscow's heyday, the so-called Silver Age, '...a cultural era of unprecedented richness and creativity, which came to a peak on the eve of the First World War';[7] a 'remarkably vibrant' period in Russia's 'cultural life' when the new and the experimental coexisted with the established and the traditional to 'make up a richly patterned and intricate mosaic of a quality and intensity which Russian artists have never been able to match since'.[8] 'From 1910 onwards', Moscow, Rosamund Bartlett writes, 'became a centre for the avant-garde – a dynamic, bustling metropolis where the most daring art exhibitions were held'.[9]

For Henriette, the heady excitement of those days meant that, for her, 'The two years in Moscow 1915 and 1916 were the most interesting time in my life'. There were concerts and recitals, operas and ballets at the Great Imperial Theatre (the Bolshoi) in Theatre Square as well as at Zimin's Private Opera. And, she wrote, 'all the theatres were just so good', from the conventional Little Imperial Theatre (the Maly) in Theatre Square to the experimental Kamerny Theatre and the renowned Moscow Art Theatre:

Life in Moscow was wonderful, the theatres, especially the Art Theatre, where we saw Chekhov's plays, and I even saw 'Knipper' (the wife of Chekhov) in the *Three Sisters*. The concerts, ballet and opera were at the height of perfection. It was really too good to last.

Founded in 1898 by Konstantin Stanislavsky and Vladimir Nemirovich-Danchenko, the Moscow Art Theatre had first moved into their famous premises in Kamergersky Pereulok in 1902. It was here that the celebrated architect Feodor Shekhtel, by skilfully and extensively remodelling the existing site, had effectively created a new building for a new style of acting.[10] 'The decor of the auditorium was similarly austere – a marked change to the gilt and velvet of traditional theatres', Rosamund Bartlett confirms.[11]

Some years later, in his autobiographical work *My Life in Art*, Stanislavsky would describe the simplicity of the interior of his theatre with its seasoned oak furnishings and white-painted walls, designed to direct the audience's attention to the stage.[12] Stanislavsky had also gone to great lengths to make sure that the Art Theatre was supplied with the most up-to-date technology:[13] an ingenious lighting system was installed and a special revolving stage was constructed underneath the main stage, with an electric trap, which could be raised to form a mountain terrace or lowered to form a river or a chasm.[14]

There was, furthermore, the Art Theatre's association with Anton Chekhov, an association that had begun with the company's successful production of *The Seagull* in 1898, only two years after the play's poor reception in St Petersburg.[15] *The Seagull* would be followed in quick succession by *Uncle Vanya, Three Sisters* and, in 1904, *The Cherry Orchard*,[16] which would prove to be his last work. But it was *The Seagull* which, while marking a turning point in Chekhov's career as a playwright, would also come to define the Art Theatre itself. And it was the seagull motif, appliquéd onto the first stage curtain, which would subsequently be repeated on all the theatre's posters and programmes.[17]

The play would also have an impact on Chekhov's private life: it had been at a rehearsal for *The Seagull* that he had first met his future wife,[18] Olga Knipper, the talented young actress whom he married in 1901,[19] some three years after their first encounter. Henriette, who saw 'all the Chekhov plays' that were put on 'in the Art Theatre', would also have seen *Uncle Vanya* and *The Cherry Orchar*d, the other two of his works which had continued to be staged.[20] But it was Olga Knipper as Masha in *Three Sisters* who really captured her imagination. This was the actress's most famous and most touching role.[21] But Chekhov's intentions not withstanding ('There was an explanation [in the programme] from the author of how he wanted the sister to be', Henriette recollected), by 1915 Masha's lines would have resonated with the pathos of the actress's personal life; Masha's loss, so movingly conveyed by Chekhov, had seemingly and poignantly become reality. For not only had Chekhov and Knipper been obliged to live apart, Anton in Yalta battling with tuberculosis and Olga, with his encouragement, pursuing her acting career in Moscow, but theirs had also been a brief marriage, abruptly terminated by Chekhov's death in 1904.[22]

There were, of course, other plays and other playwrights. Henriette would always look back with a certain nostalgia to Maurice Maeterlinck's play *The Blue Bird* (*L'oiseau bleu*), an enchanting and enormously popular work, which had first been staged by the Art Theatre in 1908.[23] A delightful contemporary design by Egorov (now in the Art Theatre's Museum) shows the two children, Mytyl and Tyltyl, together with their birdcage, silhouetted against a flock of blue birds which bear more than a passing resemblance to the theatre's seagull motif. Although no new productions were put on between 1916 and 1917,[24] during the 1915–1916 season the Art Theatre functioned more or less normally. The Russianist Harvey Pitcher has described how 'Anniversaries, always religiously observed, came and went: the two hundredth *Three Sisters* in November 1915, the two hundred and fiftieth *Cherry Orchard* a few months later'.[25] Nevertheless, there were restrictions to be circumvented: the increased tax on expensive theatre tickets, introduced in November 1915, had forced the Art Theatre to respond by increasing the number of cheaper seats available.[26]

But as far as Henriette was concerned, Moscow's cultural life was largely unaffected – 'It was so far away from the war that life was going on normally'. In the autumn of 1915, *The Musical Times* was reporting that 'At Moscow, the Imperial, the Zimin, and the People's Operas are open... From all of this it would appear that in Russia folk are by no means forgetting that there are still in this world other matters than the purely martial'.[27]

Moscow was clearly such a special place for Henriette that, on a recent visit, I decided to turn back the clock, to imagine what the city might have looked like in the spring of 1916. I would retrace her steps and attempt to add life and colour to the static monochrome world of the old black-and-white photographs.

In the early years of the twentieth century, Moscow would have been a city of contrasts: of wide boulevards and narrow cobbled streets, of eighteenth-century mansions and twentieth-century apartment blocks, of nineteenth-century public buildings so classically perfect earlier in the century and so distinctively Russian by the 1880s; a city of turn-of-the-century Style Moderne (Art Nouveau) hotels and emphatically neo-Russian railway stations.

71

I began by returning to the Arbat, to the Arbat Square of 1916. Here again there would have been a marked distinction between the old world and the new, between the sedate nineteenth-century houses and the fashionable Praga restaurant with its up-to-date interiors, between the modern motor cars and the old-fashioned horse-drawn vehicles, which criss-crossed the square from all directions. In 1916 Henriette's eye would doubtless have been drawn to the recently erected bronze statue of Nikolai Gogol. Seated on a large plinth decorated with characters from his most famous works,[28] body hunched forward, head turned to one side, the sculptor has engagingly portrayed the great writer in contemplative mood.

With the Nikitsky Boulevard to the north and the Prechistenka to the south, Arbat Square was one of a number of squares that punctuated Moscow's Boulevard Ring. From Arbat Square, I turned east into Znamenka Street, a short thoroughfare which in 1916 would have been dominated by the impressive Alexander Military Academy, the elite training establishment for the future officers of the imperial army – young cadets with uniform high-necked multi-buttoned jackets, epaulettes and tall peaked caps.

Another day I turned instead into Vozdvizhenka Street. Running directly parallel to Znamenka and Bolshaya Nikitskaya, with the Corner House (the aristocratic Sheremetev family's Moscow residence) towards one end and Arseny Morozov's exotic mansion (the home of one of Moscow's wealthiest merchants) at the other, together with the Foreign Office Archives and the impressive premises of the Economic Society of the Officers of the Moscow Military District,[29] the Vozdvizhenka of 1916 appears to have constituted something of a microcosm of the upper echelons of Moscow life.

Then out on to the Mokhovaya; a moment to enjoy the view of the Kremlin from this elevated position before crossing the road and descending into the Alexander Garden where, away from the relentless traffic of the twenty-first century, I could even now imagine Henriette walking purposefully past the flower beds and the linden trees with the tall red-brick walls of the Kremlin towering over her; past the granite obelisk, which had been placed there to commemorate the three- hundredth anniversary of the Romanov dynasty in 1913, and the Manège, 'a drill-hall for the Moscow garrison'[30] and occasional exhibition centre, which had been constructed just five years after Napoleon's defeat in 1812.

Out of the Alexander Garden, into Voskresenskaya Square, and on to Theatre Square: crowds of people walking in front of the fountain and the manicured flower beds, sitting on the benches or boarding the electric trams that ran through the square. Ladies with long skirts and elaborate hats, peasant women with knotted headscarves, businessmen in suits, soldiers in uniform. Although this vast square was still dominated by the Great (Bolshoi) Imperial Theatre, here too there would have been a marked contrast between the old world and the new, between the classical grandeur of the Bolshoi and the Style Moderne splendour of the recently built Metropole Hotel.

Just across the road from the Bolshoi and with a frontage on Petrovka Street, Muir & Mirrielees, Moscow's first department store, had recently been re-housed in a distinctive modern building with large display windows.[31] With its strong Scottish connections, with numerous departments selling clothes, toys, household goods and furniture[32] and with novelties such as 'customer lifts',[33] 'ladies' lavatories'[34] and 'a refreshment room',[35] the shop was something of a Moscow institution as well as a considerable commercial success. The store's profits, not to mention the one hundred and twenty-page catalogue which they produced for the 1915–1916 season, would suggest that at least in Moscow, as the Russianist Harvey Pitcher has pointed out in *Muir & Mirrielees: The Scottish Partnership that Became a Household Name in Russia*, the war was having 'little effect on the lives of the monied classes'.[36]

The Upper Trading Rows in Red Square was another establishment where Henriette would have shopped in the spring of 1916. This vast Russian Revival edifice, its two central towers designed to complement the historic Kremlin opposite, had first opened in the 1890s. Inside, 'three glass-covered corridors'[37] or arcades, each 'three stories in height'[38] and accessible by means of a number of internal bridges and walkways, housed hundreds of shops catering for both wholesale and retail customers. Otherwise Moscow's 'best shops', *Baedeker* tells us, were to be found 'in the Kuznétzki Most, in the neighbouring streets'[39] and in the elegant glass-roofed shopping passages such as the Petrovsky, the Solodovnikov and the Alexander Arcades.

For food, there was Yeliseyev, the leading purveyor of comestibles, with an amazingly ornate emporium on Tverskaya Street; by way of contrast, there were the market stalls and small shops on the Okhotni Ryad (Hunters' Market), which sold all manner of fresh produce.

From the Okhotni Ryad, it was only a short distance along the Mokhovaya to Bolshaya Nikitskaya. Had Henriette made her way up this historic street, lined with houses, palaces and university buildings, she would have passed the sixteenth-century Nikitsky convent (destined to be demolished on Stalin's orders in the early 1930s)[40] and the Conservatoire with its music school and concert halls, before turning into the quieter lanes with their attractive gardens.

This walk, which had taken me right through the centre of Moscow, had proved to be a poignant as well as a somewhat disturbing pilgrimage: unlike the young woman of 1916, I was only too aware that one day soon these streets would echo with the sound of gunfire and of revolution.

CHAPTER 12

CHALIAPIN

From time to time, Henriette would have returned to the country. Moscow's magnificent Vindava (Windau) Station, one of the city's nine railway stations, was the starting point for the six-hour train journey to Nelidovo, or perhaps to that part of the estate where her father had 'made arrangements for the train to stop for a moment...and let us down'.

Vindava Station was one of a number of impressive new railway stations that had been constructed in Moscow at the turn of the century. An old black-and-white photograph, taken soon after the station first opened, shows the dining hall reserved for first and second-class passengers. Although the room is, as yet, empty, the long tables are set with white cloths and waiters hover expectantly in the background. The high ceiling and refined architectural details, the candelabra and the potted palms, all conspire to lend an air of elegance to the scene. This was, after all, the age of rail travel.

Almost a century later, when I come to visit Vindava (now Rizhsky) Station I discover that a train museum has recently been opened there. Serendipitously, I find myself standing in front of a pre-war steam engine, a magnificent and to my mind rather romantic contraption. And I can envisage Henriette strolling past just such a locomotive, doing her best to avoid the billowing smoke and the grimy smuts, proceeding along the crowded platform, looking out for the distinctive blue paintwork of the first-class carriages.[1]

In the spring of 1916, Henriette would venture somewhat further afield: she would accompany her husband to Saratov, the town on the Volga where Osip's parents now lived. They would travel on one of the many passenger-steamers that navigated the river. A trip along the Volga had by now assumed the status of an iconic journey[2] and a number of companies operated these large craft, which generally offered such amenities as well-appointed cabins, a saloon and a good restaurant,[3] where, as one traveller remarked, 'even the menu is printed in French as well as in Russian'.[4] With a comfortable first-class cabin on the promenade deck and the promise of some excellent food ('caviare' and 'fish dishes' were a speciality[5]) and wine, Henriette and Osip settled down to enjoy the voyage.

It proved to be a memorable trip:

> The first night on the boat I was very disturbed by a dog barking. I rang the bell and asked for the dog to be removed. I was told that it belonged to our famous Schaliapin [the great Russian singer Feodor Chaliapin] and that the dog does not sleep when his master is not there, so I proposed that Mr. Schaliapin should go to bed. It was all very funny, and the next morning there were regrets.

Chaliapin, who was notoriously attached to his French bulldogs, was highly amused by this incident and, after a round of apologies, there then followed what were, for Henriette, several truly unforgettable days; days which she and her husband spent in the company of the celebrated singer Henriette was overwhelmed: 'He looked like a god, all in white and so tall and handsome'.

A great storyteller, who was always delighted when he found a good audience,[6] Chaliapin would no doubt have been charmed by the beautiful young woman, an aspiring singer herself, who was so clearly entranced by this encounter:

He told some wonderful anecdotes and also spoke about his work. He told us how he prepares his parts for the opera. He lives it through while studying and when he appears it is so much with him, that he has only to follow.

Chaliapin would begin by studying his own role, then, in order to gain a greater understanding of the character he had been engaged to play, he would learn the whole opera in its entirety, from the music to all the other parts as well.[7]

During the days that followed, Chaliapin could have told them how he set about physically evoking a character not only through the judicious use of make up, but also by conveying his outward presence, his demeanour, his way of moving and talking. This, as he related in his autobiography *Ma Vie*, would have required imagination as well as intellectual effort. For Chaliapin, the first step was to imagine the individual as a whole before adding the details.[8]

But, as he explained, in order to convince the audience and fulfil their expectations, he would also have to take into account the impression he was making. In his autobiography, the singer recounts how when he was first shown a set of coins depicting Boris Godunov as a clean-shaven ruler, he felt disinclined to follow their example: the Tsar was of Mongol origin and the public would expect him to have a black beard;[9] and so, as evidenced by contemporary photographs and paintings, this was how Chaliapin first portrayed him.

So much preparation: when Chaliapin was required to play a real historical personage, as in the case of Boris Godunov, he would immerse himself in the history of the period.[10] Henriette remembered that:

He spoke a lot about Boris Godunov, the part he created and it was an unforgettable performance. He promised to send us tickets and so he did. I nearly got quite crazy at the end and shouted 'Bravo'. It was not only his wonderful singing but the acting was so exciting it was quite nerve-racking. We went on to see *Boris Godunov* several times and every time it was just as marvellous and unforgettable. I don't think that anybody else could do it. His hallucination of the dead child and his own death were unique.

There was one performance of *Boris Godunov*, Henriette writes, when Chaliapin 'sang "God Save the Czar" [the Russian national anthem] on his knees, and the Bolsheviks never forgave him'. This episode, which was said to have taken place at the Mariinsky Theatre in St Petersburg,[11] would indeed have political consequences for Chaliapin, although, as Victor Borovsky points out in *Chaliapin: A Critical Biography*, the singer would later go on to claim that it was not intended to be interpreted as a political gesture.[12]

By the time Henriette and Osip met Chaliapin, he had been playing the part of Tsar Boris for almost twenty years.

From his first appearance in Russia at Mamontov's Private Opera in Moscow[13] to his success in Paris only ten years later,[14] this would continue to be his most famous role, a role he would play for very nearly forty years.[15] And yet it was one which he was constantly working on, refining, adding new touches to, endlessly seeking perfection.

A magnificent full-length portrait of Chaliapin by Alexander Golovin shows the singer attired in an elaborate costume. The artist has employed gold and silver foil to convey the richness of Tsar Boris's sumptuous robes. The distinctive Russian crown rising from a base of fur, the bejewelled fingers echoing the gems that adorn the weighty gown, all serve to enhance what is a supremely impressive portrait. This monumental work, which was executed in 1912, was based on the famous costume, apparently shimmering with rubies, pearls and emeralds, which had been designed some four years earlier.[16]

But there is another portrait of Chaliapin in this role that holds more interest for me. This time the artist is Nikolai Kharitonov and the date is 1916.[17] Chaliapin as Boris is depicted in a calf-length robe, lined in red, which lies open to reveal a plain gown encircled by a flowered cummerbund. Kharitonov has chosen to paint him without his crown. Bare-headed, deeply frowning, his reflective – even tortured – expression suggests that the historical knowledge that Chaliapin had so studiously acquired may have given him an even greater understanding of the troubled Tsar. It may well be that this was how my grandparents first saw him.

But while Chaliapin was undoubtedly famous for his elaborate make up and costumes, they were only the outward manifestation of the character that he had so painstakingly worked on; his concern would always be with his subject's inner soul.[18] Only two years earlier, *The Times* had observed that 'M. Chaliapin lives every part he plays so completely that his inaction is as eloquent as his action'.[19]

There are several portraits of Chaliapin the man as opposed to the actor. Standing in front of Konstantin Korovin's portrait of 1911, which now hangs in the State Russian Museum in St Petersburg, I am confronted by a large man dressed in a creamy white suit, a blue tie knotted loosely round the upturned collar of his shirt. It is a relaxed pose. He is leaning back in his chair, one arm resting on the nearby table. The window is open; the table is laden with some of life's pleasures: a bottle of wine, a glass, fruit, flowers. A fleeting moment, but the artist has succeeded in capturing his unmistakable attraction. And indeed his charm, his charisma, his magnetism are so apparent that I cannot fail to understand how enthralled Henriette must have been.

As they made their way down the Volga towards Saratov, their ship would have passed through Kazan, the town where Chaliapin was born in 1873. A childhood spent beside the Volga (from Kazan the family moved to Astrakhan) would leave him with a life-long affection for the river.[20] On this occasion the singer was on his way to Essentuki, a spa town in the northern Caucasus noted for its 'cold alkaline springs'.[21] He then proposed, as he wrote to his daughter Irina, to move on to the Crimea. This letter, dated 26 May 1916 (OS) and written from on board the *Goncharov* as she sailed between Samara and Saratov,[22] was, for me, a fortuitous discovery as it pinpoints the date of my grandparents' own journey.

They had set out at what one contemporary guidebook considered to be 'The best TRAVELLING SEASON'.[23]

With several embarkation points to choose from, Nizhny-Novgorod, which was about ten hours by train from Moscow, would perhaps have been the most accessible. From here, *Baedeker* informs the traveller, steamers run by concerns such as 'the *Volga Steam Navigation Co.*; the *Caucasus & Mercury Co.*; ...and the *Russian Co.*',[24] to name but a few, would ply the river. Calling at countless towns and villages along the way, their passengers would be rewarded with a series of fascinating vistas: the thickly wooded forests of the Transvolga region,[25] Kazan's exotic towers and minarets; Simbirsk, Samara, Volsk and the seemingly never-ending steppe; and, finally, Saratov, a welcoming vision of churches, 'garden-clad slopes',[26] and brightly coloured roofs — 'reds of many shades, two or three different greens'.[27]

John Hubback, an Englishman who undertook a similar voyage some two years earlier, remarked that:

>...the view of it [Saratov] from the river, whilst the boat is still some miles away, is very imposing. The town stands high above the water, and is encircled by hills which here reach some hundreds of feet above the general level of the steppe. It is a very busy scene, as the steamers are in constant motion, and of all descriptions and sizes. The barges and rafts that have no call to make at Saratoff [sic] take an outer channel, as the Volga is three miles wide here and the sandbanks are many.[28]

A reminder that the Volga was above all a working river, a commercial highway transporting great rafts of timber, steamers laden with grain and salt, tankers carrying petroleum from the Caspian.[29]

Saratov itself was a large and prosperous town with a number of fine buildings and a new university; an attractive city with green- and gold-domed churches, wide pavements[30] and captivating views of the river. And yet, characteristically, it is neither Saratov nor her parents-in-law but Chaliapin, the musician, the singer, who has become the focal point of Henriette's journey.

CHAPTER 13

A HOUSE IN THE COUNTRY

Some weeks later, Henriette and Osip left Moscow again:

While the war was on my father could not resist buying another estate of a different character. It was an agricultural place, but the most important thing was the mansion. It had been given by Catherine the Great to one of her lovers as a place for hunting and fishing. It was beautiful and my father fell in love with it. After generations it had been sold to a lawyer, who modernised it, putting in running water, bathrooms and so on.

But I must describe the house. One entered through double doors to a large hall with paintings by well-known artists. Then followed the library, a round room with excellent books, drawing-room, dining room and some more rooms. Upstairs were the bedrooms. A chapel adjoined the house with old icons. A river flowed through the grounds and there was marvellous fishing, especially trout. There were very good riding horses and one could gallop for miles.

My father bought it for me to stay there with my own family in the summer holidays, as until now we all

lived together. The only drawback was that it was
rather far from any trains and one had to go by carriage
on a bumpy road. It is very exciting for me to remember
our first visit there as unfortunately we only spent one
summer there and that was the summer of 1916.

A brief, idyllic interlude:

After that it was not possible to go back there the
following summer as there were troubles with the
militant peasants – It was a short lovely dream to have
been able to take in all the beauty of the place.
Unfortunately the peasants destroyed and damaged
everything. Each took a bit of the piano and thought
it would play. They also destroyed the icons and the
chapel was burnt down.

In March 1917, the newspaper *Izvestia*, noting the growth
of anarchy among the peasants, was already observing that
it was in Russia's best interest that the private ownership
of land should be abolished and the land handed over to
the state[1] – an editorial that only too plainly outlined the
shape of things to come.

Throughout 1917 there would be a significant increase
in the number of peasant uprisings and, as this type of
vandalism became more widespread, many manor houses
and their contents would be subjected to looting, to destruction and on occasion even to arson.[2] Henriette's description
of the fate that befell one of her beloved Steinways eerily
echoes the description of a similar incident which took
place during the Revolution of 1905 when, as Orlando
Figes relates in *A People's Tragedy: The Russian Revolution*,

1891–1924, a group of peasants had also removed a grand piano and distributed the keys amongst themselves.[3]

But the fate of Russia's many country estates had already been sealed: by the end of the nineteenth century, countless historic properties were no longer sustainable as aristocratic landowners, hampered by the emancipation of their serfs, persisted in living beyond their means. The agrarian disorders and revolutionary unrest that heralded the early years of the twentieth century also did much to contribute to the inevitable decline of the Russian country estate.[4] Discouraged by the arson attacks and vandalism which characterised the Revolution of 1905, many landowners chose to put their properties on the market.[5] In some cases vendors included their books, their furniture and their paintings, the priceless artefacts that made up the historic fabric of their estates. And indeed when my great-grandfather came to make his purchase, he seems to have acquired the entire contents of the house, from the 'paintings by well-known artists' in the hall to the 'excellent books' in the library, to perhaps even the 'very good riding horses' in the stables. In short, he appears to have bought the whole property lock, stock and barrel.

The association with Catherine the Great, assuming that Henriette was not mistaken, suggests that the attractive neoclassical manor house would have been constructed around the third quarter of the eighteenth century. Stylistically, this would fit in with her description of the library as 'a round room'. And, if the oval library, which was evidently such a significant architectural feature, was located at the centre of the house, it is likely that this room formed the nucleus of a compact plan and that the manor house itself was not unduly large, making it eminently suitable as a summer retreat.

But, in the end, there was only one summer, the summer of 1916. Regrettably, Henriette's short tantalising description is all that now remains. 'I am so very sad', she wrote, 'that I do not have any photos of the place, as all our things were confiscated'. Regrettably, too, I believe that this may well have been the last time that Henriette, Osip and Tatiana holidayed together as a young family.

CHAPTER 14

A MUSICAL INTERLUDE

When Henriette returned to Moscow she would have had to contend with the growing food problem, the persistent shortages occasioned by the war. Food was not only expensive but meat and other produce such as butter and eggs were also in short supply.[1] 'Everything started to disappear in the shops', Henriette recalled, 'and you were not sure of anything'. Soap and coffee were invariably unavailable[2] and, as the writer Stephen Graham discovered, in many parts of the city there was no sugar at all.[3] Waiting in line, forming lengthy queues, had by now become the norm and, as Graham related, there were queues for queues: 'Thus recently 2,000 waited on Arbat from 4 p.m. to midnight for a ticket for a turn next day'.[4]

And yet, notwithstanding the privations, the spirit and ingenuity of Moscow's cultural life appears to have been undiminished. Henriette's memoir offers a fascinating glimpse of the musical world, an intimate account of a close-knit circle:

Anna El-Tour had always great ideas, she thought it would be good for painters and sculptors to get to know about music and she proposed to invite them, choose one composer and perform all the vocal compositions. Several great singers promised to come and

sing at these evenings. There were also pianists, violin-
ists and cellists. First there was a small talk about the
life of the composer. All the singing was done in the
key the composer intended it.

One evening when we had the composition of Gluck,
our famous coloratura singer Nezhdanova sang a
beautiful air and the same evening I sang the mezzo-
soprano [air], 'Che faro senza Euridice'. Nobody
thought anything wrong to have on the same evening
a star and a pupil.

Antonina Nezhdanova, one of the leading sopranos of the
first half of the twentieth century, was an exceptional singer.
A soloist at the Bolshoi since 1902 (the same year that she
graduated from the Moscow Conservatoire), her rise to
fame had been meteoric: an outstanding artist who is still
revered in Russia today.

These musical evenings with their unusual approach
would no doubt have been in keeping with the dynamic,
innovative culture of the time. 'It was an ideal atmosphere', Henriette recollected, 'and the artists enjoyed it very
much, painting on while listening to music'. A remarkable
vignette which for me goes some way towards explaining
her enduring nostalgia for those Moscow days.

But aside from the intellectual stimulation, she readily
acknowledged that there were more mundane concerns:
'Food was already very scarce and everyone brought whatever
they could for the tea we were offering'. The musical world,
as Henriette's memoir suggests, was peculiarly resilient.

CHAPTER 15

REVOLUTION

By the end of October, *The Times* was already drawing attention to 'the highly charged atmosphere created by the growing food crisis'.[1] And, as Russia entered the third winter of the war, public dissatisfaction with the tsarist regime and their management of what was proving to be a lengthy conflict would be further exacerbated when 'the disgraceful mishandling of food-supplies'[2] became even more acute.

Public disapproval had, for some time, also extended to the Tsarina. Accused of being pro-German and of conducting an improper relationship with the notorious Grigory Rasputin, she had become a figure of hatred. When Rasputin's body was discovered floating in the icy waters of the Neva River, the news of his murder was widely welcomed.

'At the beginning of 1917 with the dreadful losses of the Russian army the atmosphere was changing', Henriette wrote. 'The food question was becoming more difficult. The people were disturbed by the failure of the war and the Czar had to abdicate. The whole of Russia was in a turmoil'.

In January 1917, *The Times* reported that Russia was 'experiencing famine in the midst of plenty...The scarcity of food, the general want of provisions, is the one thing felt, the one thing talked of throughout the land'. In

Petrograd, in Moscow and throughout the country, people were obliged to contend with 'an inadequate railway system' overburdened by 'the double strain of ordinary distribution to the population and the tremendous special calls arising out of the war'. Criticising 'the want of organization and coordination in all measures pertaining to the food supply', the newspaper's correspondent confirmed that '*queues*' had now 'become the rule – for meat, for bread, for milk, for vegetables, for sugar people wait in long "tails". Rich and poor participate in them, the latter in person, the former by proxy through their servants'.[3]

Matters would come to a head in February when the endless queues for bread in Petrograd sparked off a series of mass demonstrations and strikes. Within days, as hundreds of thousands of people attempted to march into the centre of the city,[4] the Tsar, unaware of the severity of the situation, ordered the Petrograd military to use force to put an end to the unrest.[5] As snipers fired from the rooftops and machine guns raked the Nevsky Prospekt,[6] what had begun as a largely peaceful demonstration rapidly became a revolution.[7] Torn by conflicting loyalties, some soldiers joined the demonstrators, others mutinied and turned on their officers;[8] less than a week after the first clamour for bread, this rebellious, violent, revolutionary activity had ushered in the Provisional Government.[9] The February Days also heralded the downfall of the Tsar, who was obliged to abdicate, thus effectively bringing to an end three hundred years of Romanov rule.

In Moscow, where the situation was altogether more peaceful, the tsarist regime appears to have fallen with 'no resistance and no fighting'.[10] 'Not a shot did we hear in connection with the February revolution', an eyewitness related, 'and as far as we know none was fired in Moscow'.[11] Despite the bitter cold, people congregated in the streets and in Red Square, where the 'crowd was thick'.[12] For Robert Bruce Lockhart, Britain's vice-consul in the city, the 'most vivid memory of that [first] afternoon was the warmth of the surging mob before the Town Duma' and the general sense of 'good-tempered confusion'.[13]

In Petrograd, the new Provisional Government appointed Prince Lvov Prime Minister; Alexander Kerensky, a young lawyer with political ambitions, was nominated Minister of Justice. Kerensky was undoubtedly the leading figure in the new government: his notoriously charismatic personality had made him immensely popular with the people.[14] When a new coalition government was formed in May Kerensky was appointed Minister of War.

He was without doubt a gifted orator. In Lockhart's opinion, 'in his own peculiar way, Kerensky must be regarded as one of the great orators of history. There was nothing attractive about his delivery. His voice was raucous from much shouting. He had few gestures... But he had words at his command and he spoke with a conviction that was all-compelling'.[15]

Moscow's Bolshoi Theatre was the setting for one of Kerensky's most impassioned speeches. 'How well I remember his...visit to Moscow', Lockhart wrote. 'On this occasion the huge amphitheatre was packed from top to bottom. In Moscow the embers of Russian patriotism were still warm, and Kerensky had come to stir them into flame again. Generals, high officials, bankers, great industrialists, merchants, accompanied by their wives, occupied the parterre and first balcony boxes. On the stage were the representatives of the Soldiers' Councils'.

After 'the usual ten minutes' delay...the buzz of conversation gave place to a burst of clapping, and from the wings the pale figure of the War Minister made its way to the central dais. The audience rose to him'.[16] Henriette too had been part of that audience: 'I myself also heard Kerensky talking in Moscow', she remembered. 'I heard him speak promising a change'.

Reginald Urch, living in Moscow at the time, has described how 'While cheers were raised again and again and clapping filled the theatre for some minutes' Kerensky, who 'had come from gruelling weeks of speeches at the front', appeared tired and 'far from heroic...A hush came, and he began to speak; but even during his speech I think he never raised his eyes to the level, to say nothing of looking up at the balconies and boxes'.[17]

A consummate performer, 'He paused for what seemed minutes, then went on to tell of what he had seen at the front. He told of heroes in the Army and heroes in the rear, of the determination of new-born Russia to continue fighting... His hearers were spellbound. They had, it was clear, expected and wanted to be spellbound, for Kerensky had then reached, if not passed, the peak of his fame and popularity in Russia'. He urged them to put aside their jewels and their luxury, to 'Sacrifice them to help, clothe and encourage our men still holding out against the enemy', men who were already 'sacrificing their life-blood for Russia'. The audience was enraptured. 'People tore off their necklets, bracelets, and rings. Some threw them on the stage; others waved them about, not knowing what to do with them'.[18]

But the people's enthusiasm for Kerensky would prove to be ephemeral. Henriette would later maintain that:

He brought a lot of distress. He made a dreadful mistake by giving the soldiers too much liberty, explaining to them that they were equal to their officers, that they are free to do what they want. They don't need to salute the officers, as there is equality.

She would have been referring to Order Number One and its successor, the Rights of Servicemen. The former, which had been signed immediately after the February Revolution, had been formulated as a means of encouraging the soldiers to go back to their barracks.[19] The basic premise of the Order, reported the French writer and journalist Claude Anet, who witnessed the February Revolution in Petrograd, was that while military discipline must be observed when on duty, in their political, social and private lives soldiers would have the same rights as other citizens; in particular, they would no longer have to salute their officers.[20] Order Number One had paved the way for the Rights of Servicemen (the Declaration of Soldiers' Rights), which Kerensky issued shortly after he became Minister of War. Once again, despite certain concessions, the new Declaration upheld the abolition of obligatory saluting by confirming that a voluntary acknowledgement would suffice.[21]

Henriette recalled that Kerensky had attempted to rally the soldiers with his charisma and the power of his oratory – 'He went to the front and spoke to the soldiers. He promised to send enough ammunition and food that they should go on fighting with new strength, but nothing arrived. The soldiers were already in a bad state and that prompted them to leave the field and run home'. There were indeed large numbers of deserters,[22] and large numbers of casualties too.

In the spring of 1917, Kerensky had travelled extensively along the Russian front[23] promoting the Provisional Government's forthcoming offensive. However, when the June offensive failed, the coalition fell apart, the disillusioned Prince Lvov resigned and Kerensky took over as Prime Minister while at the same time retaining his position as Minister of War. In August he journeyed to Moscow to attend a State Conference[24] where, despite his impassioned pleas, he met with little personal success.

For Alexander Kerensky, the Moscow Conference signified the beginning of the end.[25] In September, amidst increasing strike action in the cities and escalating violence and land seizures in the country,[26] he announced a new coalition government; it proved to be powerless, quite unable to stem the rising tide of anarchy. While the wily Lenin was promising peace, Kerensky was now being blamed for everything. As Henriette remarked, 'And so we have to thank him for all the misfortune that came upon Russia'.

On 25 October 1917, the Bolsheviks seized power in the Russian capital and the course of history was changed forever. But whereas the famous October Revolution had met with little resistance in Petrograd,[27] this time it was Moscow that bore the brunt of the violence, and this time Henriette too would be caught up in the conflict:

There was shooting in Moscow; our house was opposite the White Russian Officers' club. For ten days we could not leave the house, as the shooting was over our roof, until they surrendered.

As the fierce fighting raged between the Bolshevik forces and those who remained loyal to the Provisional Government, in the centre of the city the civilian population waited helplessly in their houses and in their apartments. Living 'at the Arbat' – and a great deal of street fighting did take place around the Arbat area – Henriette would have spent those ten terrifying days at the centre of some of the fiercest counter-revolutionary activity. Furthermore, since the family house was opposite the White Russian Officers' Club, it would have been close to both the Economic Society of the Officers of the Moscow Military District, on the corner of Vozdvizhenka and Bolshoy Kislovsky Pereulok, and the Alexander Military Academy in Znamenka. The courageous resistance exhibited by the cadets from this Academy, which was one of the principal bases of the White Guards,[28] would play a significant part in the loyalist defence.

The fighting began on the night of Friday 27 October,[29] only two days after the decisive revolution in Petrograd. Those loyalist forces, the military cadets, the officers, the student volunteers, who opposed the Bolsheviks[30] had all been organised by the Moscow City Duma's hastily-created Committee of Public Safety.[31] They would carry on fighting in support of the Provisional Government, albeit with a temporary suspension of hostilities,[32] until the Committee, ostensibly concerned for the welfare of the city's historic buildings and the lives of her citizens, surrendered to the Bolsheviks.[33]

All through that first night Henriette would have heard the sound of firing in the streets, a sound that would continue with little let-up for the next ten days. Reginald Urch recollected how 'All day and all night...except for occasional lulls, sometimes for a few minutes, sometimes for an hour or more, the din of artillery and exploding shells continued...Some nights differed from others in the luridness of the sky, due to fires, and other flashes from various causes'.[34] Boris Pasternak's younger brother, Alexander, who was living in the family apartment on the Volkhonka, just round the corner from Znamenka, remembered the relentless cacophony as the Bolsheviks manned the heavy guns which bombarded the Kremlin and the Alexander Military Academy.[35]

Henriette would have been living in the vicinity of some of the city's most strategic thoroughfares: Znamenka Street, Arbat Square and, directly to the north of the square, the Nikitsky Boulevard, the tree-lined boulevard that led from Arbat Square to the Nikitsky Gate. The Nikitsky Gate, which covered a direct connection between the Kremlin, Tverskaya and the Alexander Military Academy in Znamenka, was the scene of much intensive and persistent fighting. 'About five-thirty Wednesday [1 November] afternoon', some five days after the insurrection had first begun, the fires burning in the vicinity of this vital intersection led one eyewitness to note that 'the sky...was lit with licking flames, and a dull red glow hovered over the whole city'.[36]

The Bolsheviks fought hard, deploying machine-guns as well as rifles. This was all-out urban warfare with cobblestones ripped up to create trenches in the streets and snipers stationed on convenient rooftops.[37] The Bolsheviks even went so far as to place a machine-gun on the tower of St Andrew's Church, the Anglican Church that served Moscow's English community.[38]

Caught up as they were in the cross-fire, Henriette and the family would have had to endure what must have been a truly alarming siege – 'Nobody was allowed to leave the house', she remembered, 'a curfew was announced and food disappeared'; the telephone was out-of-order; the electricity only functioned intermittently and there was little if any water.[39] Above all, they would have had to contend with the insistent, almost-unceasing noise of gunfire and of exploding shells.

Finally, at the beginning of November, it was over and Henriette, emerging into a city already dusted with snow,[40] would have found that part of the Moscow Conservatoire had been shelled and that a number of other buildings in the immediate vicinity had either suffered considerable harm or been otherwise affected: one of the piers of Ippolitov-Ivanov's home behind the Conservatoire had been struck by a shell;[41] several bullets had penetrated the courtyard of the Sheremetev Corner House in Vozdvizhenka Street;[42] and another building on the intersection of Vozdvizhenka and the Mokhovaya had been severely damaged.[43] These scars would mar the face of Moscow for some time to come.

Debris littered Arbat Square where barricades of iron railings, wooden planks, branches torn from neighbouring trees and even a somewhat incongruous bench, had been hastily erected. When Oliver Sayler, the young American theatre critic who had recently witnessed the 'dull red glow' hovering over the city, walked up to the Nikitsky Gate, he discovered that the 'desolation was thorough. It was here that the fires we had seen on Wednesday and Thursday had burned themselves out. One of them had left a smoldering shell where a large drug store once stood… Across the street, a charred skeleton was all that remained of Moscow's finest apartment house…'.[44]

As he moved around Moscow, Sayler observed that 'Barricades still blocked the way in many of the streets. A wall built of firewood from the cellar of the Great [Bolshoi] State Theatre stood guard over the blackened ruins of the annex to the department store of Muir and Merrilees [sic]'.[45] And when he got to Theatre Square and saw the battered façade of the Metropole Hotel, the young man paused for a moment to take a photograph. This evocative black-and-white image clearly shows the extensive damage wrought by the fierce fighting of the past few days: the gaping windows, the shattered glass, 'the shell-holes and bullet splashes',[46] which now sadly defaced the exterior of what had until recently been one of Moscow's newest and finest hotels.

He would find that the 'human scars and the human destruction were even more universal'. Outside the Old University on the corner of the Mokhovaya and Bolshaya Nikitskaya, 'where the bodies of the wounded and the unidentified dead had been gathered', the long queue of people 'anxiously waiting for news of those who had ventured into the shell-swept streets and had never returned',[47] vividly brought home the true cost of the conflict. When the firing was over and '[t]he bodies of the fallen had all been removed', Reginald Urch saw that 'blood was still in the tramway grooves, and small pools here and there in the streets, as well as gruesome smears on some of the walls'.[48]

'No one will ever know what was the toll in lives',[49] Sayler remarked. But, in the aftermath of the uprising, the fate of the numerous non-combatants who had been 'killed in the street firing and in the various conflagrations' and the demise of the military cadets, the officers and the student volunteers who had perished in support of the Provisional Government would be eclipsed by the public burial of the Bolshevik fallen, who would be interred 'between the rows of trees on the far side' of Red Square, 'just under the looming northeast wall of the Kremlin'[50] (the location of Lenin's future Mausoleum).

CHAPTER 16

RED MOSCOW

Henriette had emerged into a new and very different world, a world in which so-called "class-enemies"[1] would be endlessly oppressed. Even before the Moscow insurrection Lenin had wasted no time. In the early hours of 26 October, the morning after the October Revolution, his Land Decree had announced that private ownership of land would be immediately abolished, with landlords receiving no compensation and no recompense.[2]

Under the new regime not only landowners but the middle classes too would be singled out for persecution as punitive decree followed punitive decree. Private banks would be nationalised and, with the compulsory search of safe deposit boxes, items such as gold coins, foreign currency and other valuables would be forcibly expropriated.[3] Lenin would further legitimise the continuing persecution of the bourgeoisie by declaring that it was right to share out their goods, right to take back the wealth which they had stolen.[4] The 'reign of terror introduced by the Cheká [the infamous All-Russian Extraordinary Commission for Combating Counter-revolution, Sabotage, and Speculation] very soon oppressed the citizens of Moscow like a plague',[5] one Moscow resident recorded.

In the countryside too, the peasants carried on seizing private land and property while 'Red detachments' repeatedly searched for "class-enemies".[6] Henriette herself would find that the general desire for retribution ensured that, as she put it, 'The first punishment went to the landowner'. She recalled that:

There were searches looking for my father, as land-owners seemed to be the evil of all people. One evening two peasants came to the house and explained that they have arranged to take my father with them in order to save his life. They took him away and arranged for him to rest at different places. They walked through dense woods and stayed with him until it was safe for him to leave the country and go to Riga. I think that was a marvellous way for them to show their gratitude for everything he had done for them, risking their own lives.

My great-grandfather's philanthropic attitude, his concern for the welfare of the peasants who worked on his estates, had evidently stood him in good stead.

But landowners were the not the only people who lived in fear of the dreaded knock at the door; once the house searches had begun many former officers would be arrested.[7] 'My husband', Henriette confirmed, 'had to disappear, as he was an officer of the army, and managed to get away alive'; a parting that would affect my grandparents' relationship for many years to come. 'And so', she wrote:

my mother, my sister and myself remained in the house without a man. One had to be very strong to endure all the changes. One evening about ten o'clock my little girl got a high temperature. I phoned the doctor, but there was no reply. So without any thought I put on some old clothes, not thinking of the curfew, to go and fetch him. I got through to him along small little streets and persuaded him to come over to see the child.

This incident may well have occurred in May 1918 when, following a number of disparate episodes, *Sovnarkóm* (the Russian acronym for the Council of People's Commissars[8]) declared martial law in Moscow.[9] By contravening the curfew and venturing out on to the streets at night, Henriette had risked being challenged or, worse still, arrested or even imprisoned. Later in the summer the vulnerability of the Reds would lead to martial law being enforced all over the country.[10]

Although they had initially benefited from an unexpected lifeline – 'At our house in Moscow we also got some parcels of food left on the doorstep from our peasants at [P...]. We never knew who brought them' – Henriette was finding it increasingly difficult to feed the family:

So my mother and I had to start living a strange life. There was nobody to ask for help and the condition of my room with the child was not healthy. We also did not get any food cards...

The issuing of food cards accorded with the Bolshevik policy of controlling both the supply of food and its distribution. Without the appropriate credentials, Henriette would have been unable to purchase even the most basic of foodstuffs at a reasonable price. 'The food question', she acknowledged, 'was very serious. As we did not work we were bourgeoisie

Tsar Nicholas II and the Tsarina, Libau, 23 August 1903.

Grosse Strasse, Libau, beginning of the twentieth century.

Kurhaus, Libau, *c.* 1900.

The town was a fashionable summer resort.

Bade Strasse, Libau, beginning of the twentieth century.

Frances Simson (centre) outside the House of Lords, 1908.

Suffrage procession, Princes Street, Edinburgh, October 1909.

Feodor Ivanovich Chaliapin
(*right*) in the role of Boris
Godunov, 1913.

Russian Revolution, Moscow,
1917. Barricade on Arbat
Square (*below*), 2 November
(OS). Henriette lived in
the vicinity of this strategic
thoroughfare.

Red Army soldiers entering Riga, 3 January 1919.
Henriette and Tatiana had arrived in Riga at the end of December after travelling for several days in horse-drawn open sledges.

Henriette and her daughter, Tatiana, Riga, *c.* 1920.

Henriette (*right*), date and place
unknown.

Coenraad V. Bos
with Henriette (*left*),
Riga, *c.* 1925.

Henriette (*below*)
with accompanist,
early 1930s.

Henriette's villa (*above*) at Jūrmala, *c.* 1930. The double height music room is in the middle of the building.

Tatiana (*left*) on the first-floor balcony of the villa, early 1930s.

Tatiana (*right*) at the Riga seaside (Jūrmala). Beach pyjamas were fashionable in the 1930s.

Osip, Henriette and Tatiana, Riga, New Year's Eve, 1936.

Henriette, aged eighty-one, with one of her great-grandsons.

[*burzhúi* – a general term of abuse[11]] and we got hardly anything'. They would, for instance, have had no access to the bread cards: the single sheets of paper with detachable coupons, which entitled the bearer to receive a specified ration of the coarse black bread that had by now become the staple.

Henriette was reduced to selling their possessions:

> We had to go to the market and sell small silver things or clothes for the food we needed; for silver or gold ornaments you could buy bread, meat, and fruit.

People 'bartered their trinkets, furniture, linen, and spare clothes, for we were still in the first year of Bolshevist rule, when personal possessions in the majority of homes were not yet much depleted',[12] Reginald Urch confirmed. A pitiful tableau, currently on display in Moscow's former Museum of the Revolution, shows a young woman offering a number of decorative household items for sale. With a fine lace-trimmed cloth in her hands and an assortment of decorative silver objects laid out on a blanket at her feet, she waits patiently for a prospective purchaser. A number of contemporary black-and-white photographs of similar scenes also bear witness to the level to which many people of "unsatisfactory class-origin"[13] had descended.

Under the Bolshevik regime families would also be evicted from their homes or forced to share their living space.[14] And while in Moscow the compulsory sharing of living space appears to have initially been confined to the larger apartment blocks, the compulsory requisitioning of private houses soon followed. At the beginning of March, Ivan Bunin, observing the plight of his friend Kamenskaya (the wife of the writer Anatoly Kamensky), noted that the Kamensky family had been given only forty-eight hours to vacate their apartment and remove their possessions.[15] In August requisitioning would be extended to all dwellings.[16]

The middle classes would also have had to contend with a number of other intrusive Bolshevik decrees, which permitted officials to instigate house searches and take away furniture and other valuable items.[17] By August even clothes would be nationalised.[18]

'One was not sure what the next day would bring us', Henriette remembered, 'and so it happened that one morning in the middle of the year [1918] we got a printed letter: it was the order to leave our house with everything intact, in twenty-four hours. We were not allowed to take any of our belongings, just a small suitcase of clothes and personal linen. We were ordered to an old house outside Moscow' where:

We were offered two single rooms on different floors [one] for my mother and sister, and [another for] myself, my baby [Tatiana was three years old at the time] and nanny. It was outside the town in an old and cold house with no comfort.

It was a dreadful blow to leave our dear house with all the furniture and my Steinway. My mother could not take it in, that everything was taken from her and that she had to leave her house. She became rather melancholy and had no desire to go on living. I had a difficult time explaining to her the changes in the country and to beg her to keep on looking after my sister who was still quite young.

And in keeping with the changes in Henriette's personal life, the city itself was also visibly changing as anniversaries and other public events called for innovative measures. To mark the capital's first May Day celebrations, Voskresenskaya (Resurrection) Square, adjoining the Alexander Garden, was renamed Revolution Square.[19] In the ensuing months and years, many more of Moscow's streets, squares and boulevards would be renamed.[20] Had Henriette walked through the Alexander Garden later that year, she would have discovered that the granite obelisk, which had been erected in 1913 to commemorate the tercentenary of the Romanov dynasty, was now inscribed with a roll-call of some twenty writers and thinkers who were deemed to reflect the ideals of the revolution.[21]

The first anniversary of the October Revolution had provided a more than legitimate reason for extensive celebration. Dozens of monuments and sculptures were erected; in Theatre Square, Lenin personally unveiled a larger than life-size monument to Marx and Engels. Crowds gathered in the brightly illuminated city as agit-trams bedecked with propaganda messages toured the streets, which had been exuberantly transformed by posters and banners as well as the liberal use of paint. On Znamenka Street, *Pravda* reported, the columns of the Alexander Military Academy had been painted red. Theatre Square too had been ambitiously decorated[22] and the market stalls in the nearby Okhotni Ryad had been transformed with brightly coloured paint and primitive patterns.[23]

Inevitably all the slogans, all the decorations, all the posters, all the vivid paint, did not disappear overnight. The following February, the writer and journalist Arthur Ransome (later known as the author of *Swallows and*

Amazons) commented on the 'revolutionary sculptures' and the painted 'hoardings' that he had encountered on a walk around the city, remarking that 'though the weather had damaged many of their pictures, enough was left to show what an extraordinary carnival that had been'.[24] From garish street art to pock-marked buildings, Henriette would have found that the very fabric of Moscow had been tainted by these all-too-visible reminders of the previous year's revolution.

CHAPTER 17

FLIGHT

The autumn of 1918 saw the escalation of the infamous and relentless Red Terror. The unsuccessful assassination 'attempt on Lenin's life [he had been hit by two bullets[1] after addressing a workers' meeting at a Moscow factory[2]] had evoked a new outburst of Red Terror',[3] Reginald Urch recalled. From the beginning of September people lived in constant fear as 'searches and arrests were going on all around'.[4] More unsettling still was the Cheka's predilection for working through the night. 'That was the habit of the Cheká at this period. We already knew, from trustworthy hearsay, they would pounce upon a house, pluck victims here and there from their beds, and march them off to spend the rest of the night on the cold floor of some prison...'.[5] Many of these victims would go on to be summarily executed.

From the autumn onwards, day-to-day life in the city slowly deteriorated. It was a harsh winter, significantly colder than the previous one.[6] Moscow was deep in snow,[7] fuel was scarce, the streets were unlit,[8] and the conditions under which Henriette was forced to live were also infinitely worse – 'There was no heating nor water and we all got ill. But life went on' – and it must have been a truly dreadful existence as they struggled to cope with the lack of running water, the poor sanitation and the cold, damp, unheated rooms.

107

Above all there was the daily struggle to obtain food, which was 'already very scarce in Moscow'.[9] They ate what they could, however unappetising, such as the coarse dark bread, at times bulked out with wheat-husks, potato or even straw.[10] But, as prices soared, the cost of such food as was available could on occasion be astronomical. Hungry and cold, sometimes ill, they were living on a hand-to-mouth basis, always fearful that their under-nourished, unhygienic way of life might lead any one of them to contract scabies[11] or one of the more serious infectious diseases, such as typhus,[12] which flourished in Moscow that autumn.

It was now that Henriette's concern for her daughter's welfare led her to approach Anna El-Tour:

> I went to see my dear friend El-Tour and she promised to help me to leave the country. Apparently she belonged to the musical society that was formed to look after the artists. They were asked to recommend a singer to go to Riga and meet the Russian army, when they occupied the town, and entertain them. She suggested me as I knew several languages and although I was not quite ready for concerts, I seemed to be the right person.

It was by no means unusual for singers to be employed in this way: from July 1918 onwards, music had been consistently used to encourage the fighting forces.[13] By the following spring, over a thousand musicians would be performing for the soldiers at the front.[14]

In the middle of December the Soviet newspaper *Izvestia* triumphantly proclaimed that the Red Army was freeing Estonia and was nearing Valga. With the border town of Walk (Valga)[15] not much more than 12 miles away, they were fast approaching Latvia. The Bolsheviks were intent on profiting from the uncertainty following the November armistice to take possession of the Baltic states.[16] By the end of December, *Izvestia* was going so far as to suggest that Estonia, Latvia and Lithuania were hindering the revolution by separating Soviet Russia from revolutionary Germany and to advocate the conquest of the Baltic states and the Baltic Sea as a means of facilitating the spread of social revolution.[17]

For Henriette, the opportunity 'to follow the Red Army and entertain them' was clearly a proposition that required serious consideration: 'After talking it over with my mother I decided to accept the offer, but insisted that the papers should be properly signed by the authorities'. Since the whole object of the exercise was to be issued with the necessary papers and food cards this was obviously of the utmost importance:

> I had no other choice, as the health of my little girl deteriorated and I had to save her. It was a very sad farewell with my mother and sister, as we were not sure whether we should ever see each other again. My nanny was very energetic, packed whatever she could, put some money in her case and distributed a few jewellery pieces that we dared to take. Our papers were all ready and we left Moscow, not knowing at all whether we should reach our destination.

On 20 December, Henriette, together with Tatiana and her nanny, boarded the train which:

> ...should have taken us to Riga. But halfway through our journey two armed Bolsheviks and a woman came

into our compartment, asked for our papers and started to strip my clothes and took away everything: my money, jewellery, and whatever they liked. Luckily they did not touch the child and nanny. They told us that we are arrested for taking money out of the country. They took us to a private house and there we stayed without anybody looking for us.

After a week I went to the police to enquire why we were kept in this village when all my papers were in order. They were quite puzzled, as they did not know anything about it. Apparently a gang of hooligans (some impostors, pretending to be the Red Army) went through the train and took away everything.

They had in fact been targeted by one of the armed gangs who habitually roamed the country,[18] thieving and looting as they went.

We had lost a whole precious week and alas the trains did not function any more. The police tried to help us and suggested that they would arrange for us to continue in sledges. They arranged two sledges with two horses each. I sat in one with my child as near my body as possible. They gave us old rugs and coats and we started our journey in the middle of winter.

With the countryside shrouded in snow – 'It was the end of December and it was very cold' – blinding blizzards and gale-force winds would have made the next stage of the journey a daunting prospect.

The first day was not too bad. We arrived in the evening and no one wanted to let us have a room. They did not accept the Bolshevik money. We were starved and frozen. I heard some music coming from a hall; I went over and asked for an officer to talk to. They [the Red Army soldiers] were very happy to see me and thought I would sing for them. I explained to the officer the situation and he went with me. After a few words we were given a room, a fire was lit, and we also got some hot tea. He promised to come to see us in the morning and see how we were getting on.

I was so grateful; he brought us a little bread and *two* hard-boiled eggs. He accompanied us out of the village but could not go further, as one did not know where the army was. We were in no-man's land without any protection. After a few hours we were told by some soldiers that we can't use the road at daytime, as the army is expected to come. We reached another little village. There was not a soul. Everything was locked and there was no shelter. We had to travel at night. There were flares of light in the sky, and the peasants who drove us said we had to turn back as the Devil was after us.

It was not uncommon for superstitious peasants such as these to believe in the 'numerous spirits' or 'devils' who, they were convinced, brought 'disease, temptation and every conceivable misfortune' in their wake.[19] Meanwhile, huddled in one of the open sledges, Tatiana's fourth birthday came and went as she watched her mother carefully rationing out the two hard-boiled eggs:

...the only food I could give to my child during the four days and nights of our gruesome journey. In small little crumbs I pushed in her mouth half an egg per day. We had nothing to eat. Throughout all these four days we did not see a living soul. I am sure they were all in hiding and nobody opened the door for us.

More than half a century later, Henriette would confess that as the days went by she could not help thinking:

Was that the right thing to do? But I had to save my child as the conditions in Moscow deteriorated so drastically that I would not have been able to get any milk or other food necessary for a child, and so I took the chance to leave the country.

By the winter of 1918–1919, 'the food problem had become acute in Moscow'.[20] Bread and milk were often unobtainable and, one English resident noted, 'Fats of all kinds had become rare luxuries. People cooked with fish-oil, bought from chemists'. They ate frozen, even half-rotten, potatoes and 'occasional horseflesh', which had by now become a staple product, 'handled with gloves for fear of glanders [an infectious disease contractable from horses], then common in Russia'.[21] The medical situation was just as worrying: as more and more people succumbed to typhus, hospitals had become so overcrowded that if patients did succeed in being admitted they were lying two to a bed or even on the floor.[22]

Henriette would always be conscious of the immense debt of gratitude she owed to Anna El-Tour who had, after all, facilitated her escape. As for El-Tour herself, when the violinist Albert Jarosy visited Moscow some two years later, he would find that her spirit was apparently undimmed:

> Cold and hungry, the 'People of Yesterday' sat in their ruined homes... They went foraging in the morning for the provisions that were becoming ever rarer; they heated their stoves with broken-up furniture or with books. It was the winter of 1920.

> But Anna El-Tour, the singer, had, it seemed, not lost her enthusiasm... 'Would you like to hear some new songs of Nicolas Carlovitch's [Medtner]?' she wrote. 'He is going to accompany me himself! Come to tea, and bring a few bits of wood with you, if you have any'.[23]

CHAPTER 18

RIGA 1919

When Henriette set out from Moscow in December 1918 the future of Russia's former Baltic provinces was still very much at stake. Earlier in the year, when Germany, together with Soviet Russia had signed the Treaty of Brest-Litovsk, the wording of the treaty had left no doubt as to Germany's desire to maintain and expand her sphere of influence in the east.[1] And in November, despite her ostensible defeat in the Great War, Germany's ambition to exert control over the greater part of the Baltic region was seemingly undiminished.[2]

But whereas the signing of the armistice had effectively marked the cessation of hostilities on the Western Front, on the Eastern Front the continuing threat posed by the Red Army remained very real. The immediate solution was to allow German troops to remain in Latvia for as long as they might be required,[3] a decision not without its own inherent dangers.

To further complicate matters, on 18 November 1918, just one week after the signing of the armistice, Latvia declared her independence. Four days later[4] a British naval squadron was sent to the Baltic in order to 'help to strengthen the populations of that part of the world against Bolshevism' and 'assist British interests there'.[5] Sailing under the command of Rear-Admiral Alexander-Sinclair, they were instructed 'to show the British flag...and to support British policy as circumstances may dictate';[6] a somewhat vague remit, which at times would be freely interpreted.

When the Sixth Light Cruiser Squadron reached the Gulf of Finland in the middle of December they found that the Red Army was already approaching Tallinn (Reval). Alexander-Sinclair responded to the gravity of the situation by bombarding a number of Bolshevik positions to the east of the Estonian capital;[7] an action that might be construed as a somewhat liberal interpretation of his original orders. He then proceeded to accompany the *Ceres*, the *Princess Margaret* and two of his destroyers through the Gulf of Riga to the Latvian capital,[8] where he left them under the command of Captain Smyth.

By the end of December, the situation in Riga was entering a critical stage. 'PANIC AT RIGA', *The Times* reported. 'The Bolshevists are approaching from the north of the town. Many families are fleeing from fear of massacre and from anxiety lest they should be inscribed on black lists'.[9]

When Henriette finally reached her destination a new and terrible series of events was already beginning to unfold:

We arrived in Riga on the 31st of December. We went to my parents' flat, which was being looked after by some of his office people. I noticed that the streets were crowded with British sailors. I rushed down and asked them if they were going to defend the city. They assured me that we can sleep in peace.

Only a day or two before Henriette's arrival there had been great consternation in Riga when two regiments of

Latvian soldiers had threatened to join the approaching Red Army, who were rapidly advancing on the Latvian capital. Once the British navy had agreed to intervene, the *Ceres* had opened fire and shelled the army barracks which housed the offenders.[10] 'The mutineers', the Admiralty was informed, 'had subsequently surrendered, and British patrols were keeping order in the town'.[11] And, indeed, on the night of 31 December, Captain Smyth recorded that while 'considerable firing, including machine gun fire, was heard in various parts of the town towards midnight...no serious disturbances occurred'.[12]

But that night it was of course Tatiana, weak and severely dehydrated after her ordeal, who would have been the focus of Henriette's attention: 'The first thing we had to do was to get a doctor as my little girl was in a very bad state. He came very soon and ordered one spoonful of milk or soup every hour. She was starved. It took three weeks to get her a little better'.

On 1 January, as Henriette anxiously nursed her small daughter, the British shore patrols continued to operate. However, when Alexander-Sinclair sailed into Riga harbour the following day, he ordered the patrols to be withdrawn that night and instructed his ships to make ready to sail for Copenhagen at daybreak.[13] It was becoming obvious that the Bolshevik advance could not be halted and that the city would soon fall. Despite their promises, no help from the Germans had been forthcoming[14] and, as the Bolsheviks approached, the Germans, who were clearly reluctant to comply with the terms of the armistice, had themselves begun to withdraw from the town. And so, much to Henriette's dismay, 'The next morning the warships left and the Russians entered'.

On 3 January 1919, soon after noon, the Red Army marched into the city[15] and Latvia became a Soviet Republic. Her new masters wasted no time in issuing a number of punitive decrees. George Popoff, who was living in Riga at the time, has described how within hours the streets had been plastered with posters displaying the directives of the new Soviet government.[16] In the coming weeks a plethora of rules and regulations would follow. Innumerable house searches would be conducted, possessions would be confiscated and private property requisitioned. And once food supplies were controlled by the Soviet, food cards would be issued.[17] As 'no food was allowed to be sold either in the shops or in the open market',[18] when provisions became scarcer, it was the bourgeoisie who would suffer most.

Fortunately for her, Henriette's role as a singer for the Red Army afforded her a certain degree of immunity from many of these stringent measures:

I was given a lot of privileges as an artist: a notice on the door that I am not to be searched, and cards for the child and ourselves as working class people.

Our life was going to be easier and quite soon I started to appear in the afternoon at a café frequented by soldiers. I always started my concert with 'Divinités du Styx', a very difficult air. A dear old pianist who used to play for all the great artists wanted to give me some courage and came to play for me. Of course I also sang some easier songs for the soldiers and they were very happy although our repertoire was not exactly light music.

117

To all intents and purposes these were Henriette's first public appearances. Only a year or so earlier, on the memorable evening when Antonina Nezhdanova had been present, she had chosen to sing Gluck's *Che farò senza Euridice*. Now she had turned once again to Gluck, to another of his powerful operatic works, *Alceste*, and the moving aria *Divinités du Styx*, in which the protagonist addresses the agents of death, the Deities of the Styx – the mythological river that divides the earth from the underworld.

The Bolshevik regime was evidently committed to bring music to the people. Artists would perform in factories ands barracks, in crowded concert halls and workers' clubs.[19] Even the great Chaliapin remembered singing in a military riding school before an insalubrious audience of several hundred workers.[20] As a young student, Henriette surely could never have envisaged that one day she would be obliged to make her début in the somewhat unlikely surroundings of 'a café frequented by soldiers'.

Day by day, week by week, as more and more decrees and regulations were issued by the Soviet, large numbers of people were shot or died of starvation[21] or from infectious diseases such as "spotted typhus";[22] while the Bolsheviks occupied Riga thousands of people would lose their lives. Shooting was the most common form of punishment and many of the victims were summarily executed in a forested area on the outskirts of the city.[23] Henriette recalled how 'During the five months of occupation by the Red Army a great deal of people used to disappear at night, never to be seen again. The atmosphere round me was very morbid'.

As the intrusive house-to-house searches persisted people sought ways in which to protect their belongings. They endeavoured to conceal their jewellery, their silver, their furniture and even their food in ever-more ingenious hiding places, or implored friends and acquaintances to take care of them[24] and, once clothes, shoes and linen had been requisitioned in February,[25] these too became valuable possessions. Presumably because she was protected by her 'card' and by 'doing some work for the soldiers, some people', Henriette wrote, 'tried to bring their valuable things to be safe in my flat'. But, ever mindful of Tatiana's welfare should something happen to her, she felt compelled to refuse – 'Unfortunately I could not risk it, as I would have been shot immediately', she admitted.

However, when she was able to help without jeopardizing their safety, she could be generous:

> One day an Estonian Baroness brought some valuable pieces of jewellery to sell to me. They needed money desperately to escape but one had to pay a big price. I had to persuade her to borrow some money from me (money which the nanny had smuggled through from Moscow, and it was quite substantial) and to keep the jewellery for worse days as she had six children. They promised to repay and as soon as they settled down, after about two years, she sent the money; they were free and well.

Throughout the long months of occupation, when her work for the Red Army was her lifeline, Henriette's commitment never flagged:

> The atmosphere was very tense and everybody was afraid. I continued to sing every day from five to seven o'clock and had enough time for my own study.

Sometimes I had to go to another town, but was always back the same day. After a few months I was allowed to give a concert, sharing it with a Russian pianist.

At our last concert...we heard some cannonade. German and Lettish armies [Lettish troops and Baltic Landeswehr supported by the Iron Division[26]] combined came to liberate the town. The Russians left in great haste not to come back until 1940. There was great jubilation.

Riga was liberated on 22 May 1919[27]. By the end of the day exultant crowds had flocked to the Esplanade where, according to one eyewitness, in their eagerness to eradicate all evidence of their Soviet occupiers, they wasted no time in tearing down and unceremoniously destroying all the plywood structures, the obelisks and plaster monuments which had served to commemorate the heroes and thinkers of the revolution. As night approached all the images, all the insubstantial trappings of the former regime had gone up in flames.[28]

But although, to the great relief of the population, the Bolsheviks had wasted no time in fleeing, the inhabitants of the city would find that they had only exchanged one form of persecution for another. Within days Major Fletcher (the Governor of Riga and a notorious Prussian officer) had announced a state of siege;[29] martial law was imposed and a strict curfew was enforced. Under Fletcher's draconian rules, anyone venturing on to the streets after 6 o'clock in the evening without police permission would be subject to the death penalty. According to Lieutenant-Colonel du Parquet, who made a copy of Fletcher's proclamation, a number of other infringements, such as the possession of a private telephone, carried the same terrible punishment. The proclamation also made it clear that should anybody at any time dare to fire on the occupying troops from any house whatsoever, all the residents of that house would be forced to pay with their lives.[30]

'The people are in great fear of the Germans, who rule the town with iron discipline', Lt Colonel H. R. Alexander (the future Earl Alexander of Tunis) informed the Foreign Office at the beginning of June.[31] The new occupation of Riga would later be denounced as 'a veritable reign of terror', with the British Foreign Office claiming that the Governor had taken the opportunity 'to execute large numbers of Letts, under the pretext that they were Bolshevists'.[32]

'No one knew what the situation was going to be', Henriette acknowledged:

I felt that we should leave Riga at once. It was not so easy, as many other people wanted to do the same. One had to get a special permit to leave the town but the great difficulty was to get a ticket for the train to go to Libau and also there was only one train daily. Luckily I knew the man who was in charge and got my permit at once but he could not help in getting the tickets. It was pretty hopeless.

In the evening the nanny and myself sat on the balcony of our flat, watching the soldiers marching though the streets. There was a severe curfew and no one was allowed on the street after 6 o'clock in the evening. One nice German officer passed our house and suggested that I should come down and have a drink

121

with him. I reminded him of the curfew and he apologised and asked if he could do something for me. I was delighted and told him about the ticket difficulty and he very kindly offered to arrange it for us.

He was very eager to help, and he really came the next morning with the train ticket and a car to take us to the station. I simply could not believe it. There were hundreds of people queuing. He, with his Iron Cross on his chest, went through with us at once, seated us in the train in an empty compartment, waited till the last minute, kissed my hand, took off his Iron Cross and gave it to me and said that he would like me to think that they [the Germans] are also human.

It took me some time to take it all in.

CHAPTER 19

LIBAU 1919

As her train steamed out of Riga, Henriette would no doubt have marvelled at the Iron Cross which had been so surprisingly handed to her by her unknown German saviour. Although by 1918 this distinctive medal had already been awarded to several million soldiers,[1] it was one that would none the less have been worn with pride, and Henriette could not fail to have appreciated the unexpectedly gallant gesture.

'At last we reached Libau', she recollected, 'which was actually occupied by the Germans during the whole of the war. [The former Russian port and naval fortress had been captured in the spring of 1915]. When I arrived I had a difficult time and had to take a lot of responsibilities. My old nanny was tired and could not stay with us; I had to engage a young nurse and Tania had to get used to her. There was one good thing: my father's office was still working on a small scale and they were very helpful in arranging some rooms for us to stay and they also gave me a substantial allowance'.

In the months following the Soviet occupation of Riga, Libau had somewhat unusually not only acted as the head-quarters of the German army of occupation (under the command of General Rudiger von der Goltz),[2] but had also provided a refuge for the Latvian Prime Minister

Karlis Ulmanis and the newly formed Latvian Provisional Government.[3] This unfortunate coincidence had resulted in a bizarre state of affairs: in the spring of 1919, a month or so before the liberation of Riga, a number of Latvian Balts, tacitly or otherwise supported by General von der Goltz, had carried out a *coup d'état*.[4] The Latvian Provisional Government was overthrown and a new and unrepresentative government, a puppet government primarily composed of Latvian Balts, was installed.[5] In the middle of May, the head of the British Mission in Libau would report that the 'Present injustice' was 'nothing less than German Military Dictatorship'.[6]

The *coup* had taken place on 16 April. 'The situation on shore in the last two or three days has become somewhat disturbed', Rear Admiral Walter Cowan had noted rather laconically that morning. Anticipating trouble ahead, the previous afternoon he had sent a destroyer into the naval harbour 'to lie there alongside the Lettish S.S. "SARATOV"…until she could raise steam and shift to where', as he put it, 'she would be less likely to be interfered with by the Germans'. Cowan went on to recount how, while the *Saratov* was being escorted out of the naval harbour, the Germans had raided the headquarters of the Latvian Provisional Government and disarmed all the officers. Baltic German troops had then surrounded the Government offices and arrested two ministers[7] before looting the building and blowing open the safe.[8] Ulmanis, who by chance happened to be near the British Mission at the time, was able to take refuge there. The Latvian Prime Minister would later transfer to the *Saratov*, which was anchored with Cowan's squadron in the outer harbour where she was protected by the British warships.[9]

Shortly after the events in Libau, the *Times* special corre-spondent in Paris had perceptively summed up the gravity of the situation. 'The plan of the German Army Command', he wrote, 'is very clear and simple. By pretending to fight the Bolshevists, and by preventing anybody else from doing so, they maintain their hold on the Baltic Provinces. Thus they are carrying out the historic German ambition to own the Baltic littoral and so handle the wealth of Russia which comes to the sea through the ports of Reval, Riga, Windau, and Libau'.[10]

In the middle of June Marshal Foch, the supreme Allied commander, ordered the German Government to withdraw their forces from the Baltic states.[11] But although Germany failed to comply with this ultimatum, General von der Goltz did at least evacuate his troops from Libau – only to set up new headquarters further inland, at Mitau (Jelgava).[12]

By the end of the month, Ulmanis was free to disembark from the *Saratov* and return to dry land. Commodore Duff, who witnessed the occasion, reported that 'Mr. Ulmanis made his official landing on Friday 27th June, and received a great ovation from a very large crowd, the proceedings including an official reception on landing, speeches from the balcony of a hotel, and finally a concert in the evening'.[13]

On 7 July, Ulmanis and his government returned to the *Saratov* and set sail for Riga.[14] Some ten days later, the people of Libau celebrated the peace. Duff observed that on 'the date of the official peace celebrations, the ships were dressed over all, and in the afternoon a very successful sports meeting was held on shore…A band was hired, and the local officials with their families, the Lettish officers, and the French and American officers were invited. A very large number of men were landed from our own ships. Tea was provided for about 600 men and also for the officers and official guests. The afternoon appeared to be a great success. In the evening a short display of fireworks was given by the ships'.[15]

Henriette recalled that:

When the Germans were leaving Libau, some American officers opened an American centre in one of the hotels. The mother of my friend invited some officers for tea and we got to know them. There was a school friend of mine who studied piano in St Petersburg and was a serious pianist. She offered to play for me and we decided to give a joint concert. We thought it would be a good idea to invite them [the Americans] and I went to see them and took some tickets for them. They were delighted.

After quite a lot of rehearsals the day came when we had to appear before the public. I was quite terrified; the hall was packed and we had a great success, as there had been no concerts for a long time.

One American Major came after the concert and said to me that I must go to America... I told him that I was not ready yet and that I would need another year in Berlin to study. The next day at lunch with him, he quite seriously offered to help me as he had good connections in the musical world. I had to promise him to write to him as soon as I reached Berlin and keep in correspondence with him. I was not quite sure if he really meant it and did not think very much about it.

These American officers would almost certainly have been working for the American Relief Administration, which had been operating a Food Commission in Libau for several weeks.[16] Charged with distributing food to the war-torn peoples of central and eastern Europe and headed by Herbert Hoover, the future president of the United States, the ARA, which was based in Paris, comprised prominent personnel from the United States Food Administration in Washington as well as a staff of over a thousand American officers.[17]

Although I was aware that Henriette and Osip had been leading separate lives, I had never fully appreciated that her return to Latvia had marked the end of their marriage. While I shall never know why my grandparents parted so soon after their romantic elopement (had their enforced separation placed too great a strain on their relationship? was Osip disconcerted by Henriette's musical ambitions? or was he perhaps convinced that his wife and daughter would never leave Moscow?), I do know that within months they had obtained a swift and conclusive divorce.

With the collapse of her marriage, there was little incentive for Henriette to remain in Latvia. 'After a few months in Libau', she wrote, 'I knew I could not stay there, as there was no possibility of getting proper tuition. My aim', she admitted, 'was now to get to Berlin to make a serious study of the German Lieder, which was very important to me. After staying in Libau for over two months, I started to try to make arrangements to reach Berlin. Trains were not going directly and it was difficult to travel'.

On 1 August, Marshal Foch issued another ultimatum; once again the German Government failed to comply.[18] With Germany still intent on pursuing her interests in the Baltic states, General von der Goltz and the German military authorities were proving singularly reluctant to evacuate the region. And even though Germany had been explicitly banned from sending additional troops to Latvia,[19] on 6 August, the Chief of the British Military Mission in Berlin confirmed that small groups of German soldiers were seen to be leaving almost nightly from the city en route to the Baltic provinces.[20]

Moreover, as the railway lines which ran through northern Lithuania were still apparently in the hands of the German military authorities,[21] it would have been difficult for Henriette to travel to Berlin. So when, sometime in the middle of August, the American Relief Administration officers were being recalled from Latvia[22] and she was unexpectedly offered another means of transport, she unhesitatingly accepted the proposal:

> The Americans invited me and my friend to dinner and while we were discussing the situation one of the officers spoke about going by car to Berlin. I told him about my difficulties and he offered to take us with him. I had decided to take my little girl with me, as I could not bear a separation.

> The next day his chauffeur came to inform me that they would collect me tomorrow. It was a terrible rush but I could not lose such an opportunity. I spoke to my father's manager and he promised to send me a monthly allowance so that I could study in peace.

CHAPTER 20

BERLIN

Henriette's arrival in Berlin had coincided with a new chapter in Germany's history: the formal proclamation of the Weimar Constitution. This momentous event, which took place on 11 August 1919, had been preceded by an intensely volatile year. From the Kiel mutiny of the previous autumn to the abdication of the Kaiser and the uprising that had culminated in the assassination of Karl Liebknecht and Rosa Luxemburg, the country had endured an uneasy period of political instability and revolutionary unrest.[1]

Although Germany now had a new government, the legacy of the recent upheavals would have been only too apparent: the pock-marked buildings, which bore witness to the turmoil of the preceding months; the wounded and disabled veterans whose pitiful appearance served as a constant reminder of Germany's defeat in the Great War; the miserable beggars whose plight tragically highlighted the gravity of the current economic situation. Disturbing images which still evoke the harsh reality of post-war Berlin.

'It took a few days to organise our lives there', Henriette remembered; 'I had to find a proper pension for us with facilities to have a piano and be able to practice several hours a day'. And, she added, 'I had to get a kind of governess for Tania, also one had to register at the Police' – all foreigners arriving in Berlin were required to report in person to a police station within twenty-four hours.[2]

When it came to finding a governess for Tatiana, Henriette would have to bear in mind that her four-year-old daughter was only able to speak Russian. 'Luckily', she recalled, 'the girl I had engaged came from Estonia and so she spoke Russian. They went to play every day in a playground with German children and of course Tania picked up the language very quickly'. Tatiana also inadvertently benefited from the current social idealism:[3] the state's assumption of responsibility for the welfare of mothers and children[4] ensured that, much to Henriette's astonishment, her daughter was given 'the same rations as the German children'.

Before the Great War, Berlin had been the third largest city in Europe; by 1922 it would have the second highest population on the continent. The hotels, the banks, the insurance companies, the businesses, which had been established in the second half of the nineteenth century and the early years of the twentieth, reflected the solidity and seriousness of a burgeoning metropolis, which for nearly fifty years had been the capital of a newly unified Germany. But to visit Berlin was also to recognise Prussia's former greatness. In the Tiergarten alone no less than thirty-two statues of Brandenburg-Prussian rulers, all carved from Carrara marble, lined the Siegesallee.[5] Nearby, the Brandenburg Gate, that distinctive symbol of former Prussian supremacy, led to the Unter den Linden, one of the glories of Berlin. To walk along this wide boulevard, lined with lime and chestnut trees, was to embark on a mile-long roll call of German and Prussian history: the handsome equestrian statue of Frederick the Great, the elegant eighteenth century Opera House, the palaces, the libraries, the monumental Baroque Arsenal. And yet, one only had to cross the famous Schlossbrücke and confront the monumental bulk of the former Royal Palace (until recently the Kaiser's Berlin residence) to be reminded that Germany was now a republic.

Despite the city's many attractions, Henriette 'did not want to waste any time'. She would allow few distractions. She had, after all, come to Berlin with the intention of improving her voice and acquiring a new repertoire:

I had the name of the German professor with whom I intended to study. Eva [Katharina] Lissmann was a very fine German *Liedersänger*, and [I] started to work with her immediately. She was a pupil of the famous [Raimund von] Zur-Mühlen – all the great singers went from time to time to study with him. Unfortunately I did not meet him (he went to live in England), but got all the benefit from his pupil. He said a wonderful thing: that there should be a small painting of each song. It lasts only a short time and one has to tell the whole story, that the audience should take it in, otherwise it would be dull.

Henriette continued to study with Eva Lissmann, albeit on her own terms:

I did not want her to do anything about my technique, and after I met several people I got the name of a good Italian singing professor, and to him I went. It was the best thing I could do. I started my regular lessons with both professors and everything went well.

> The Italian professor asked me to come at ten o'clock
> for my first lesson and I was there punctually, to his
> dismay. My lesson was actually at twelve o'clock, but
> he expected a Russian person to be late!

With her customary energy and perseverance, Henriette had established a new life for herself, a life primarily focused on the advancement of her musical education. But events in the outside world, the vagaries of politics and conflict, would soon disrupt her plans.

The German military authorities, exhibiting a conspicuous disregard for Marshal Foch's ultimatums ordering them to evacuate their troops from the Baltic states, were still demonstrating their reluctance to abandon their position in the region. In the autumn of 1919, a fresh development saw German troops join forces with the White Russian officer and adventurer Pavel Bermondt-Avalov. Ostensibly undertaken as a justifiable step in combating Bolshevism[6], in reality this alliance was intended to further German interests in Latvia. At the beginning of October, Bermondt-Avalov's forces attacked Riga, 'bombing the town from aeroplanes and bombarding it with heavy artillery'.[7] But although the round-the-clock bombardment of the city persisted into November, the decisive action taken by Latvian troops, together with the assistance of Allied warships, succeeded in halting any further advances. On 4 November, Bermondt-Avalov turned his attention to Libau.[8] Once again Allied naval intervention was instrumental in ensuring that Libau 'was cleared of the enemy'.[9]

Ever since her arrival in Berlin, Henriette had been financially dependent on the 'substantial allowance' she received from her father's office. This arrangement was effectively disrupted when Bermondt-Avalov's troops, acting on instructions from the German capital, took control of the railway lines that ran from Tilsit in East Prussia (now Sovetsk in Kaliningrad) across Lithuania and into Latvia.[10] Once again she would have to rely on her own ingenuity in order to provide for herself and her daughter:

> After a few months the communications with Libau stopped and I was not able to get my allowance. It was quite desperate, I had a lot of expenses and we had to live. In my Pension there were some actors. One of them told me about the opening of a Kunstler Cabaret (Art Cabaret). He advised me to go and see them. They were doing two one-act plays with top artists and wanted a singer between the acts. They engaged me and I started to go every evening between nine and ten thirty to sing a few songs. I could hardly believe my luck, as I earned enough for all my expenses. It did upset a little bit of my work, but there was no alternative.

'The Kunstler Cabaret', Henriette acknowledged, 'was a great success'. However, as she soon discovered, there were certain difficulties involved in attempting to combine this engagement with the reality of caring for a small child: '… every evening when I had to go out Tania started to cry and it was agony to leave her. I had to change my Pension and move to another place, where there was a young daughter. She stayed the evenings with the child'.

The first art cabaret or "café artistique", the *Chat noir* (Black Cat), a small tavern in Montmartre where intellectuals and artists met and performed their works, had been a

Parisian phenomenon in the 1880s. In turn of the century Berlin, impresarios such as Max Reinhardt and Ernst von Wolzogen had introduced one-act plays to the repertoire as they began to explore the parameters of cabaret. Catering for an increasingly broad clientele, Berlin cabaret would go on to include parodies and political satire, vaudeville or variety shows (which derived from nineteenth-century English music hall) as well as popular revues.[11]

Whereas before the fall of the monarchy in 1918 public performances had been subject to censorship,[12] by the time Henriette arrived in Berlin the lack of regulation was undoubtedly having an adverse affect on the propriety of a number of these performances. In November 1919, in a bid to halt the decline, the SPD (Social Democratic Party) Minister Gustav Noske introduced the enforcement of midnight closing,[13] an authoritative measure, which may well explain why Henriette was able to finish her engagement at 'ten thirty', and a distinct advantage if her 'art cabaret' was in Berlin's somewhat dubious pre-war entertainment district, Friedrichstrasse. This colourful area, which the artist George Grosz famously peopled with a cast of dubious characters (cruel caricatures of bowler-hatted businessmen, society ladies, lewd prostitutes, soldiers, beggars and match sellers), also boasted a number of more reputable places of entertainment, such as the famous Wintergarten variety theatre.

But while cabaret represented the populist facet of the artistic life of the city, Berlin was also the cultural as well as the administrative capital of Germany[14] and there were other more conventional forms of entertainment. New venues such as the Deutsches Opernhaus in Charlottenburg and Max Reinhardt's vast ultra-modern theatre, the Grosses

Schauspielhaus, were constructed in order to satisfy the public's increasing appetite for the performing arts.

As for music, the Philharmonie in Bernburger Strasse, just south of Potsdamer-Platz, had for several years been the home of the famous Berlin Philharmonic Orchestra and its renowned conductor, Arthur Nikisch. Austro-Hungarian by birth, a gifted musician and a former orchestral violinist, Nikisch had begun his conducting career in 1878. After crossing the Atlantic in the late 1880s in order to take charge of the Boston Symphony Orchestra, he had returned to Europe where, among a number of other appointments, he had taken up the post of conductor of the Philharmonic Concerts; a position he would hold from 1895 until his death some twenty-seven years later.[15]

A highly respected guest conductor, both at home and abroad, he had accompanied the London Symphony Orchestra on their historic tour of North America in the spring of 1912 — the fortuitous occasion when they had narrowly missed sailing on the *Titanic*'s ill-fated maiden voyage.[16]

'An important meeting', Henriette recalled, 'was with Arthur Nikisch, to whom I had a letter from Anna El-Tour'. El-Tour had known Nikisch for some years: shortly after making her London début in 1908, she had appeared with the LSO at the Queen's Hall, where Nikisch was conducting a concert performance of the first two acts of *The Wreckers,* an opera by the English composer Ethel Smyth.[17]

The great conductor was known to champion young soloists, both vocal and instrumental, and Anna El-Tour would have been confident that he would be sympathetic to her former pupil. 'He was charming', Henriette recollected, 'and asked me to all his concerts and to see him afterwards'.

Small in stature, nattily dressed, Arthur Nikisch was by all accounts an agreeable man and an immensely popular conductor.[18] Although his conducting style was apparently quite controlled, he evidently succeeded in maintaining a unique rapport with his orchestra. Nevertheless, despite his legendary self-control, Henriette noted that, 'When he came out at the end of the concerts, he was in a dreadful state of emotion'.

Henriette would also have been present at the historic evening, in March 1920, when, in order to commemorate his twenty-five year tenure as conductor of the Berlin Philharmonic Orchestra, Arthur Nikisch had somewhat nostalgically chosen to replicate his début programme of 1895.[19] 'A wonderful concert', she remembered, 'when he had his son as a soloist'. And indeed this time, instead of a young Josef Hofmann, it was Mitja, the conductor's talented twenty-year-old son, who was at the piano.

To Henriette's delight, Arthur Nikisch agreed to give her an informal audition:

He kindly offered to hear my voice and arranged for the small concert hall [the *Oberlichtsaal*] to be opened for this occasion. He came and played a few songs that I brought with me and said that, among a hundred voices, he would recognise my voice and that made me very happy. He tried to persuade me to change over to opera, as he could arrange for me in one of the small theatres to study the opera parts. He thought it would be better than to lead a gypsy life and travel from town to town. I did not have any feeling for the opera and only dreamed of song recitals all on my own with my accompanist.

While she was clearly gratified by this reception, Henriette was, characteristically, still determined enough and focused enough to want to pursue her own particular dream.

For almost a year she had been writing to Major E[...], the American officer who had been so taken with her concert in Libau, telling him about her life in Berlin:

...and I got some charming letters from him. He said we should correspond, as that would make it easier to get a visa to America. At the beginning of the summer I got a telegram from an American impresario asking me to meet him in Hamburg. I sang to him and he emphasised that in inviting me, under his auspices, he ran a certain risk. I quite agreed with him.

I had a serious conversation with my German professor. She told me that it would be impossible to take Tania to America as I would be travelling most of the time, and if illness should happen—what then? Luckily my mother had returned from Moscow and my parents were back in Riga and wanted to see us very much. The only thing that seemed to be sensible was to take my little girl to Riga and leave her with my mother and a governess. It was not an easy decision but I was used to that.

I came back to Berlin on my own and started to prepare for my trip to New York. I had no difficulty at the American Embassy. I brought my bundle of letters from Major E[...] and was given a visa in no time. I was not too happy about all these arrangements as I felt I could have done a little more work.

Henriette had been presented with an enticing opportunity. After so many set-backs, she must have felt that this time she had been given a second chance. And, indeed, her decision to leave five-year-old Tatiana behind and set out for America, with the sole intention of furthering her career, shows how ambitious she must have been and how very keen she was to succeed.

CHAPTER 21

AMERICA

At the end of October, Henriette was ready to leave for New York. Her papers were all in order (as a divorced woman, she had reverted to her maiden name) and Tatiana was safely settled in Riga with her governess. She had arranged to sail from Denmark, a relatively long passage: after departing from Copenhagen, the ships of the Scandinavian-American Line would first put in at Christiania (as Oslo was then called), before turning to the west. 'The voyage was quite pleasant', Henriette wrote, but 'I was not in a happy mood, as I did not know how things were going to work out'. She was, after all, embarking on a distinctly uncertain future.

And with some eleven days at sea, she would have had more than enough time to reflect on the breakdown of her marriage. Indeed, when I recently discovered that Osip had married again in the summer of 1920, only a few months before Henriette left for America, I could not help wondering whether her decision to cross the Atlantic had to some extent been prompted by this crisis in her private life.

Over a year had passed since the concert in Libau which had led to Henriette's chance meeting with Major E[…]. Now, much to her relief, he had arranged for his elder brother to meet her ship. As for the Major himself, a former lawyer, he had returned to the city after the war only to find, as Henriette put it, that he 'did not wish to go back to stuffy rooms and took up farming in some wild part of America, where they also trained wild horses. He did not want me to come to see him', she rather charmingly observed, 'as he thought it would not be suitable for a young lady'.

Since the Major no longer lived in New York, 'His brother, an old gentleman, tried to look after me, showing me round the picture galleries and I was also his guest at the Stock Exchange, the famous place in New York and the loudest'; a memorable experience in the heady days of the early 1920s, nearly a decade before the infamous Wall Street Crash. Guests would usually be invited to visit one of the special viewing galleries from where they could survey the "floor". While 'the scene in the Exchange' was generally orderly and well conducted, in times of crisis, the 'confusion and excitement' in the great trading room was described by one contemporary writer as 'something that will remain in the spectator's mind for a lifetime'.[1]

Outside, in the streets of New York, the noise and the tumult would no doubt have been even more overwhelming: from the blaring horns and pulsating engines of the dashing new motor cars, to the distant throb of the subway, and the pervasive insistent rumble of the electric trains on the elevated railway – a veritable cacophony which, I imagine, New Yorkers would have regarded as evidence that their city was a truly modern metropolis.

In 1920, New York was embarking on the decade that would come to be known as the Roaring Twenties. This was the city that would so entrance F. Scott Fitzgerald that it would become the mecca to which his heroines aspired: young girls who hankered after the expensive clothes enticingly displayed in the windows of the fashionable shops on Fifth Avenue, after gleaming apartments on Park Avenue and dinners at the Ritz. These were the girls who yearned for the pulsating excitement of the Jazz Age, the frenetic escapism of post-war New York where, even in 1920, the recent introduction of Prohibition had done little to mar the gaiety.

An enticing city, a city of bright lights, from the brilliance of the electric signs of Broadway's theatre-land, where reviews and musical shows played to appreciative audiences, to downtown Broadway and the illuminations of the Woolworth Building, at some fifty-five storeys high the tallest inhabited building in the world.[2]

New York had long enjoyed an active music scene as evidenced by the number of concerts, recitals and operas that were performed in the city each year. The Philharmonic Society, the New York Symphony Orchestra, the Boston Symphony Orchestra and the Russian Symphony Orchestra were among those orchestras which held a series of concerts during the season. And, of course, there was the acclaimed Metropolitan Opera.

While the concerts given by the Russian Symphony Orchestra ensured that New Yorkers were familiar with and enjoyed the works of the Russian composers, several Russian musicians and singers had also been among the many distinguished European artists to cross the Atlantic. In the past few years New York had had the privilege of welcoming such notable performers as Feodor Chaliapin, Anna Pavlova and Sergei Diaghilev's company of Ballets Russes dancers.

The thoughtful Major had arranged for Henriette to stay with a friend of his, 'the widow of a Director of a Musical

Journey [sic]' who, she recalled, 'was still in the middle of all musical events. She was very charming and kind and made my stay with her a very happy one. I kept my rooms with her all during my time in America. She was a great help to me and took me to all the musical parties and I got to know a lot of people'.

There was the memorable evening when Henriette came across the great Neapolitan opera singer, Enrico Caruso:

I met Caruso at a musical party and he spoke to me for a while, asking many questions about my education. He pointed out to me that posture was an important asset. I thought it was very sweet of him to show me exactly the right position for my right foot and also [to] emphasise that one should always sing from your heart, which I actually did.

And indeed, when advising young singers, Caruso would invariably stand quite erect, placing one foot slightly in front of the other, as though he was about to take a step forward.[3] A convivial, likeable, generous man, he was immensely popular in New York, where he had already appeared more than eight hundred times. Shortly after this occasion, on Christmas Eve 1920, Caruso would give what would turn out to be his final performance at the Metropolitan Opera House.[4] Some six months later he died in Naples, at the age of forty-eight.

It was at another of these parties that Henriette met a musician who would have a marked influence on her career:

One evening I saw the famous accompanist Coenraad V Bos to whom I had a letter, but did not dare to approach him. I was introduced to him and he kindly suggested that I should come and sing for him. That was the happiest encounter for me as he became my accompanist and I went...to work with him and to arrange programmes for my coming concerts.

Some twenty years older than Henriette, Coenraad Valentijn Bos, who had spent the past two decades touring extensively in America and in Europe, was without doubt one of the most well-known and distinguished of accompanists. With a career stretching back a quarter of a century, he was justifiably proud that, for his first professional engagement at the age of twenty, he had played for Raimund von Zur-Mühlen, the great Lieder singer who had once been a pupil of Clara Schumann. As a young man, Bos had himself been accepted as a pupil by Schumann's widow[5] and, had she not died before he was able to benefit from this opportunity, he too would have been able to claim an unbroken connection with one of the greatest Romantic composers of the nineteenth century.

For Henriette, working with Bos 'was like a dream, as he was the most wonderful accompanist... We started to work hard. I went twice a week for rehearsals and he gave me a lot of courage. He was quite marvellous. Having played for so many great singers he could certainly teach me a lot'. Henriette knew that she was fortunate to have met him and she was determined to profit not only from his immense experience but also from his reassuring presence.

It was on her arrival in New York that she would first use her newly adopted stage name, Henriette Safonoff, a name that her impresario had no doubt devised as a means of drawing attention to her Russian heritage. He was evidently astute enough to realise that in the aftermath of the revolution a young Russian singer, previously unknown in America, would have had a certain curiosity value. And for those New Yorkers who were already familiar with Russian music and musicians, he may well have been hinting at a possible connection with the late Wassily Safonoff, the former Director of the Moscow Conservatoire and one-time conductor of the New York Philharmonic Orchestra. When it came to priming the press, American impresarios were notorious for being economical with the truth.[6]

Henriette was being promoted as a singer who had a facility for languages. Her repertoire of Russian songs included works by Mussorgsky, Dargomyzhsky and Rachmaninoff. In German, her wide range encompassed not only Hugo Wolf but also Wagner. In all, she sang in five languages, an accomplishment that would later be favourably commented on by the critics. The *New-York Tribune*, while praising the quality of her mezzo-soprano voice, would point out that 'Another feature of her equipment was her diction, which was excellent in French, English, Italian and German'.[7]

Much to her surprise, she became newsworthy:

I must also mention the reporters, who were following me and asking many questions about Russia and Europe. I was quite overwhelmed, as I had never spoken to a reporter. Each one wanted some different information, which I was not very willing to give. I was rather a shy person and did not want all the fuss. At last my landlady invited them all for a drink and we had a friendly conversation. At the end she said, 'why don't you write about her personality, her looks and her whole being?' I was medium height with dark hair, big brown eyes, slim and photogenic.

I have before me an old photograph: a beautiful young woman, seductively swathed in white, looks directly at the camera. Her hair falls becomingly onto her forehead in a series of fashionable waves and her large eyes betray a beguiling sense of mystery. A tiny logo in the left-hand corner of the image reveals that this is the work of Apeda, a New York studio, which specialised in theatrical photography. This glamorous publicity portrait, taken to promote her forthcoming concerts, is one of the few surviving photographs that I have of my grandmother as a young woman.

Her canny impresario had arranged for her to undertake an extensive tour: 'I started to sing in small towns to get the feeling of the American audiences. I did not have Bos for these concerts and had to rely on local accompanists. That meant several rehearsals with strange pianists'.

By the middle of February, Henriette had travelled as far south as New Orleans. Her arrival elicited a flurry of attention from the local press. 'The newspapers reporters', she complained, 'nearly drove me mad. Everyone wanted to know something new and there was a great demand for me to tell them all the news'. So voracious were these journalists, so keen to hear about her life and her experiences during 'the war and Russian Revolution' that many of their stories were wildly exaggerated: 'RUSSIAN SINGER TO BE AMERICAN', 'TAKES OUT FIRST PAPERS TO BECOME CITIZEN OF U.S.'[8] ran one headline; 'Henriette Safonoff, Favorite in Russia, Makes American Debut Here'[9] ran another; 'Mme. Safonoff Relates Stories of Atrocities by Bolshevists'[10] trumpeted the indefatigable reporters.

'I stayed in New Orleans nearly three weeks', Henriette recollected, 'and gave some concerts in smaller places [in Louisiana], reaching them by car'. She found that New Orleans 'was half French', with a famous old French Quarter, the Vieux Carré, as well as a French Market, a French Opera House and a club, where 'I was asked to make a speech in French telling them shortly [briefly] about my experiences'. And when 'I needed several elegant evening dresses, I got hold of a French woman who did the most wonderful frocks for me'.

Her visit would culminate with a widely-publicised appearance in New Orleans itself, 'the first big town' on her tour. Billed as 'MME. Henriette Safonoff EMINENT RUSSSIAN DRAMATIC MEZZO SOPRANO',[11] she had been contracted to give a concert at the Jerusalem (Shriners') Temple on St Charles Avenue; with a large auditorium, this was one of the city's premier venues.[12] 'My concert in New Orleans', Henriette observed, 'was of great importance: it could make me or break me. I had to get some good reports to open the door for New York's début'.

Having resolved to present her audience with a wide and varied programme, Henriette had decided to open her recital with Gluck's dramatic Baroque aria, *Divinités du Styx*, before turning to Lully, Wagner and Hugo Wolf. She would then go on to perform works by two contemporary American composers, John Alden Carpenter and Walter Kramer, before, and this was clearly a selling point with the local press, devoting the final part of the evening to the Russian repertoire: Dargomyzhsky, Mussorgsky and two songs by Gretchaninoff, whose evocative *My Native Land* conjured up the wild, elemental beauty of the Russian countryside.[13]

This was Henriette's first major concert and the waiting, the relentless attention and the high expectations of those around her, had evidently proved to be something of an ordeal: 'In her opening numbers', the *Times-Picayune* commented the following morning, 'she was visibly nervous, but as the concert progressed she gained confidence'.[14] Nonetheless, the newspaper generously went on to add, 'Mme. Safonoff' had 'at once interested her audience by her personal charm, and her fine stage presence, so that her hearers were in sympathy with her from the start'.[15] Henriette was delighted:

It all went very well and the friendliness of the people was quite marvellous. My impresario was beaming and now he was sure that I could tackle New York. And my concert in New York was advertised with Coenraad Bos at the piano.

But with her New York recital scheduled to take place in the spring, she was obliged to carry on touring, travelling in and out of the city, appearing in one town after another, following an overly demanding itinerary, one that she was afraid might be detrimental to her voice – 'All in all I sang much too much'.

It was not until Monday 11 April 1921, at 3 in the afternoon, that Henriette finally made her début at Aeolian Hall, the famous concert hall on 42nd Street. With a smaller seating capacity than Carnegie Hall, the city's other principal concert venue, the Aeolian would have been ideally suited to Henriette's first appearance in New York.

In order to give herself the opportunity to demon-strate her fine vocal talents as well as her linguistic abilities, Henriette had elected to perform another varied programme,[16] one that she had chosen in conjunction with Coenraad Bos, who would accompany her at the piano. Perhaps inevitably, she had decided to start with Gluck's *Divinités du Styx*, the powerful aria from his opera *Alceste*, the aria with which only two years earlier she had sought to entertain the soldiers of the Red Army in Bolshevik Riga, the aria with which she had begun her all-important concert in New Orleans.

There then followed a wide-ranging selection of songs, delivered in Russian, German, French and Italian. Once again, she charmingly complimented her American hosts by including the American composer John Alden Carpenter's *When I Bring to You Colored Toys*. And, as she had already done in New Orleans, she drew attention to her Russian heritage by concluding her recital with works by Mussorgsky, Dargomyzhsky and Rachmaninoff.

From the Baroque to the contemporary, from Gluck and Lully to the Chicago-based composer John Alden Carpenter, from the religious intensity of Rachmaninoff's *The Lord is Risen* to the secular rhythms of Mussorgsky's *Hopak*, it was a well-crafted programme. Moreover, the inclusion of *Schmerzen* (*Agonies*) and *Träume* (*Dreams*), two songs from Wagner's *Wesendonck-Lieder*, confirmed that the composer's works were once again acceptable to a New York audience. In the autumn of 1917, anti-German sentiment had led the General Manager of the Metropolitan Opera House to announce that Wagner's operas would no longer be performed that season; a ban that had subsequently been extended.[17] And when the opera house did stage Wagner's *Parsifal* in February 1920, less than a year before Henriette's arrival in America, the production had been given in a specially commissioned English translation;[18] no operas would be sung in the German language until the 1921/22 season.[19]

To Henriette's delight, the critics were impressed. While *The Sun* praised the subtlety of her 'reading of Hugo Wolf', the 'delicate charm' which 'she lent' to John Alden Carpenter and the depths 'she plumbed' in her rendering of Wagner and Rachmaninoff, *The World* claimed that it was in the Russian songs that she 'caught the native spirit of Mussorgsky's "Hopak" and Dargomyzhsky's "Lovely Maiden"'.

Among the many excellent reviews she received, *The World* remarked that 'Henriette Safonoff, mezzo-soprano, of eminence, showed much promise. Her voice is of lovely quality…and her musical intelligence is a fine asset'. 'Miss Safonoff Displays Fine Mezzo Soprano'; 'Voice Warm in Color Revealed in Recital', the *New-York Tribune* reported. 'Miss Henriette Safonoff…displayed much promise at her first recital in America yesterday afternoon at Aeolian Hall. She has an unusually fine mezzo-soprano voice, warm in color and wide of range. Her ideas of technique are sound and she is highly gifted as an interpreter'.[20]

Although she was encouraged by all the complimentary reviews, not to mention the ensuing publicity, Henriette understood that she was still on the threshold of her career. As the music critic of *The Evening World* elaborated, 'This singer radiates intelligence and when further experience shall have added…to her already fine vocal endowment, she will be able to command'.[21]

The Aeolian Hall recital led to a joyful reunion: 'Major E[…] came to see me for my first concert. It was a very happy meeting… He also arranged a dinner party after the concert to meet his friends...He only stayed a few days as I was very busy by that time'.

Henriette had begun to accept engagements to give 'concerts in private houses', an entertainment favoured by some of the wealthiest members of New York society: 'The rich hostesses had a concert in their houses before dinner, and that was well paid. They all wanted me, I suppose, as a novelty and my impresario made a lot of money out of me'.

But the intensity of her schedule was beginning to take its toll: 'I was singing too much and it became a great strain. Coenraad Bos spoke to my impresario, telling him to slow down – but he would not hear about it'. Twenty-seven years old, seriously concerned, as was her accompanist, that her 'young voice' should 'not be strained', she found that she was just another commodity: 'I was told that in America one does not care about young or old singers' health'.

American impresarios were inclined to overwork their protégées and under the terms of her contract Henriette would have been obliged to fulfil all her engagements:

Working hard the whole time and always being dressed with great care made me quite tired. I also had to attend some special functions. My impresario started to make suggestions that I should take a flat in an expensive hotel. Here we had a serious disagreement, as I told him he was not to interfere in my private life and that I should stay where I was.

There were other issues too:

I had weekly letters from my mother telling me about my little girl [Tatiana was now six years old] and that it was difficult for her to give enough attention to her. She was asking me to return as soon as I could manage. I never thought that I would stay in America for ever, it was too far away from my family and I was getting homesick. In other circumstances I should have stayed for a few years, as everything was so promising for me. I even had an audition at the Metropolitan, although I said that I was not interested in opera. The famous Italian Director [Giulio Gatti-Casazza] tried to persuade me to go to Italy for a year and study the parts.

By the summer of 1921, Henriette had begun to make a name for herself – 'It was a terrific experience and I got so much surer of myself having given so many recitals'. Highly motivated and singularly determined, she had always refused to be constrained either by marriage or by motherhood. But now, as she acknowledged, she would have to think again:

After my concert in New York, which was sold out, I had decided to leave for home…. Of course it was no easy decision to leave America where I had been received with so much kindness. I spoke to Coenraad Bos, who had become a real friend, and told him that I was very homesick. He pointed out to me that if I broke my contract I would never be able to sing again in America. Nevertheless I made up my mind to go back to my child and start a normal life.

'And so', Henriette concluded, 'I left America with no regrets'. Yet all the indications were that, at twenty-seven years of age, she had been on the threshold of a promising career. Among the newcomers who appeared in New York that spring, ran a report, Henriette Safonoff was one of the most successful, 'her beautiful voice, her intelligence and her musical temperament fascinated her audience'.[22]

After all these years, I could not help wondering just how much she had in fact given up.

CHAPTER 22

BETWEEN THE WARS

Coenraad Bos proved to be a tower of strength. A regular passenger on transatlantic crossings between New York and his homeland, 'Coenraad B', Henriette recalled, 'helped me with all the arrangements and even asked his friends in Holland to meet my boat'.

Two days later she was in Riga: 'I arrived in July, at the seaside, at my parents' summer home and was so happy to see them all. Tania looked well and it was a very happy reunion' – a characteristically brief comment, which once again masks the true depth of Henriette's feelings. Indeed, the stoical nature of her writing, her natural reluctance to reveal too much about her private life, occasionally raises some tantalising questions. And there was at this time one development that she seems to have been particularly anxious to conceal: the painful truth that her former husband had again become a father. Her intrinsic reticence has ensured that I shall never know how deeply she was affected by the knowledge that her return from America had coincided with the birth of Osip's new baby daughter.

Henriette has been altogether more willing to write about her professional life, about her desire to promote her career and establish herself in Europe where she hoped, as she put it, 'for a continuation, where I left off in America'. In 1923, to her 'great joy', she heard that Anna El-Tour had managed to escape from Russia via the Far East and 'was teaching in Berlin. I could go to her', Henriette explained, 'and go through my programmes and as she knew my voice so well she could always find something small which could be made right. It was wonderful to have her there, as she was a real friend'.

A gifted teacher, Anna El-Tour would invariably encourage her pupils to seek the quality of tone that best suited their own particular voice. Some years later, in the mid-1930s, El-Tour, who was now teaching in Paris, published a short book (*Conseils sur L'Art du Chant*) in which she set out her advice on the art of singing. Describing herself as a '*chanteur-musicien*', who has been interested in vocal techniques from an early age, El-Tour enumerates what she considers to be the three basic essentials of the art of singing: quality of tone, breathing and diction. The aspiring vocalist is instructed how to breathe, how to control the diaphragm and how to prepare for silence with the lungs full of air. A silence which, she insists, should not be taken as a cue for the singer to rest but should be accorded as great a rhythmic value as the sung note.[1]

Although Anna El-Tour clearly wished to pass on her expertise, as a consummate artist in her own right she continued to perform throughout the 1920s and 1930s, no doubt putting into practice her own didactic advice. 'This artist, who is a teacher of singing at Berlin', *The Musical Times* noted, 'affords an exception to the rule by proving that she is really familiar with the technical and aesthetic demands of her *métier*'.[2] Some ten years later, when the same publication's London reviewer praised her 'well-nigh perfect' breath-control, he claimed that 'It was impossible to see her breathe, or even to see how and where she breathed'.[3]

And when she gave a recital at London's Wigmore Hall in January 1939, *The Sunday Times*, impressed by her rendition of songs by Schumann and Hugo Wolf, commended her as an exceptional Lieder singer.[4]

Henriette, meanwhile, awaited another of her mentors, the accompanist Coenraad Bos:

> As soon as C. B. arrived from America we could start rehearsals. My first concert was in Dresden with Bos at the piano – he used to play half the year in Europe and the other half in America. It was quite wonderful to have him with me as he was so well known and esteemed everywhere. It was difficult to get him all the time but he did his best for me and gradually I got good audiences and could go from town to town before reaching Berlin. Of course there was quite a lot of competition but once a German audience accepted you, you were made.

And Berlin was a fitting goal. By the 1920s the city's three opera houses and their conductors, Erich Kleiber, Bruno Walter and Otto Klemperer, had put Berlin at the centre of European musical life. Together with the prestigious Philharmonic Orchestra, which, after the death of Arthur Nikisch in 1922, had been taken over by Wilhelm Furtwängler, these supremely talented conductors and their musicians vied to outperform each other.[5] Berlin had become a city that catered for all tastes, from classical music, to daring revues, to the newfangled jazz; Arthur Nikisch's son, Mitja, would combine his role as a classical pianist with his passion for jazz when he became the leader of a dance band.[6]

By the mid 1920s the stabilisation of the mark[7] had, albeit temporarily, put an end to the crippling inflation that had characterised post-war Berlin.[8] The crowded café terraces on the Unter den Linden spoke of a new ease. Contemporary photographs show young women in knee-length, loose dresses and fashionable strap shoes, their freshly bobbed hair peeking out from under modish cloche hats. These dashing young women would no doubt have appreciated the exhilarating transformation of media culture: the posters, the magazines, the brightly lit advertising hoardings, the radio broadcasts transmitted from the Vox-Haus in Potsdamer Strasse and the moving images projected onto the city's cinema screens.[9]

Henriette, who had been contracted to make her début in Berlin with Coenraad Bos, recognised that:

…it would be difficult to be acknowledged by a German audience. There were many well-known Lieder singers and one had to be very good indeed. The competition was great and I had to use all my willpower to try to succeed. The impresario had to try to fill the hall with invitation tickets, as nobody would attend a concert of an unknown singer in Germany. I had quite a lot of friends there and one rich friend of mine, she was a portrait painter, had arranged a reception after the concert for seventy people and they also attended the concert. The important thing was to get the critics to come as it depended on them very much for a future as a *Liedersänger*. Of course there is something individual in each voice and one must have the ability to bring it out. There were some notices about my American success and the critics were interested.

A selection of reviews from some of the leading newspapers of the day reveal that, by 1925, the German press had also begun to recognise her ability. They praised her musicality, the richness of her voice, her command of languages and her charm. Perhaps most encouraging of all was the critic who predicted that 'her youth' promised 'a great future'. It was, after all, a professional future to which she now aspired.

In the early 1920s, Henriette took her first flight. By the end of 1921, with commercial air travel still in its infancy, a through passenger service was already operating between Berlin and Riga.[10] Henriette may well have flown to the Latvian capital in a Junkers F.13, the new civil aircraft that had been developed shortly after the war. Carrying up to four passengers in a small covered cabin fitted out with comfortable chairs, these all-metal monoplanes[11] admirably illustrate the dichotomy between the supposedly luxurious and yet undeniably primitive nature of early air travel: the stylishly dressed pioneering woman traveller would have had to mount a low flight of steps and clamber onto the aircraft's wing before entering the passenger compartment. Always adventurous, Henriette would have relished the experience.

No sooner had Henriette succeeded in re-establishing her career than the somewhat complex nature of her private life once again came to the fore: by the middle of the 1920s my grandparents had rekindled their former romance. And, indeed, when I discovered that they had begun living together before Osip had formally divorced his wife, I was not entirely surprised: from the young girl who eloped in 1914, to the single-minded music student, Henriette had invariably shown herself to be daring, unconventional, strong-willed and determined. By the end of the decade, my grandparents had remarried.

Henriette had come to understand that, in order to attain the domestic happiness that had so far eluded her, she would have to find a way of reconciling her role as a wife and mother with the demands of her career. A career which, she explained, 'My husband encouraged...as long as I spent the holidays at home'. By accepting this condition, and by ensuring that Tatiana was well cared for while she was away, she was able to reach a satisfactory compromise: 'My mother's German governess, who was with my mother for fifteen years, came back to stay with me. She was the most suitable person to look after Tania. I did not have to worry about the household, as we had a good cook and housemaid, and everything went smoothly in my absence'.

The contentment that Henriette found during these inter-war years has, perhaps inevitably, led her to gloss over much of this period. It was a good time, a time when every aspect of her life had apparently been resolved. She had accepted the limitations on her career, she had established a new relationship with Osip as well as with Tatiana and, after so many upheavals, after so much uncertainty, she did at last have a permanent home.

And so we are left with a series of fleeting impressions: the security of life in Riga between the wars; the spacious family flat in a distinctive late Art Nouveau building in a sought-after quarter of the city; the summer residence at Dzintari, as Edinburg was now called. Specially commissioned by my grandfather, the latter was particularly dear to her – 'a gorgeous villa at the seaside, half an hour from Riga, with a music room on two floors. It was so convenient for practising and the acoustics were marvellous'.

The double height music room, which lay at the heart of the building, was, she recalled, 'furnished with antique furniture and carpets. It was ideal for entertaining'. An old black-and-white photograph reveals a room with an exceptionally high ceiling: the large expanse of wooden parquet floor is covered with a fine carpet and a few pieces of Biedermeier furniture stand in front of the tall arched windows, which have been dressed in some sort of sheer fabric. Another photograph shows a substantial house of classically pleasing proportions, the distinctive semi-circular entrance surmounted by a balustraded balcony.

My mother's sparse family album yields a number of other images: a Riga schoolgirl leaning nonchalantly against the white-painted balustrade of the first-floor balcony; a sporty teenager in a vest top and a pair of wide-legged trousers, playing in the garden, enjoying the freedom of the summer holidays; an attractive young woman sitting on a wicker sofa, elegant in a flowered summer dress. And always, in the background, the tall pine trees, which are so characteristic of this area.

The Riga seaside or Riga Jūrmala (the former Rigascher Strand), was well known for its excellent strawberries, which were grown locally in large numbers, and my grand-parents' garden was no exception. As a child, I never tired of hearing about the squirrel who 'used to come for a visit each day at twelve o'clock to have some strawberries. She was so punctual', Henriette would tell me, 'that we knew the exact time'.

When I first drove out to Jūrmala in 2001, I was relieved to find that the whole area was still relatively unspoilt. The long beach, the firm white sand, the tall pine trees, the houses and the villas were all as I had imagined. Though the grass was overgrown and weeds flourished in the once immaculate gardens, I felt sure that I would find my grandparents' house; this time I not only had a few precious photographs, I also had an address. But, to my dismay, when I got to Dzintari I realised that the house had gone. Whereas much of Jūrmala had survived in a sort of dilapidated time-capsule, Henriette's beautiful villa had been pulled down; the house that had meant so much to her had been replaced by an unappealing modern edifice.

In her role as a professional singer, Henriette also occasionally appeared in her homeland. The 'remarkable concert hall' at the House of the Blackheads had, she recollected, 'a marvellous atmosphere'. Located on the first floor[12] of one of Riga's most prominent buildings, the walls were lined with 'portraits of' the country's former 'Swedish and Russian rulers',[13] including a striking equestrian portrait of Catherine the Great 'astride a white charger'[14] – a far cry from the Riga café where Henriette had once entertained the Red Army.

'Riga used to be very famous as a musical centre', Henriette wrote, 'and all the great artists that used to go to Russia, to St Petersburg, used to stop in Riga and give some concerts'. By the 1920s the situation had reversed. Henriette remembered the 'musical evenings when whoever came to Riga, [such] as Piatigorsky the cellist, and several Russian pianists who were able to leave the country, joined us. Among them was Simon Barer, who stayed for some time in Riga and played very often for me'.

Gregor Piatigorsky, the Russian-born virtuoso cellist, had dramatically escaped from the Soviet Union by swimming across the river Sbruch.[15] Simon Barer, the talented pianist and Rubinstein prizewinner, would spend a few years in the Latvian capital before moving to Berlin; he eventually settled in America where he enjoyed a highly successful career.

Although Henriette would perform regularly elsewhere in Europe, she has confined herself to picking out one or two of the more unusual episodes. Willem Mengelberg makes another appearance, the same Mengelberg whose Museum Concerts Henriette had attended when she was a student at the Frankfurt Conservatoire, the famously irascible conductor who had so publicly quarrelled with the critics, the conductor who was renowned for his 'somewhat ruthless methods at rehearsals'[16]:

Sometimes one gets in a funny position, as once I was asked at the last moment to replace a singer who had to appear with Mengelberg in Frankfurt and sing two songs by Wagner with orchestra. As it happened I had sung them quite often and adored them. I arrived just for the last rehearsal and had no opportunity to do some practising in the morning and was rather tired. I was greeted not very friendlily by the conductor. He could not get over the fact that a young Russian was sent to sing Wagner, he was furious. I decided just to indicate the songs at rehearsal, not to sing them, as the concert was the same evening. He stopped in the middle and told me, in front of all the musicians, that he couldn't hear me. I told him that I was just listening to the orchestra.

I kept quiet, had a good practice and rest in the afternoon and was fresh and in excellent voice in the evening. I had a glamorous dress and was prepared for Mengelberg. As I had sung in Frankfurt before, I had a good crowd to receive me with great applause. He never gave me a sign to begin but I watched him and

was able to start at the right moment. I began to sing
and Mengelberg, who never looked at me, started to
smile. The orchestra gave me a wonderful reception
and it all went off very well. At the end he kissed my
hand and was hoping to see me again. I somehow
never forgot it but it taught me a lesson never to arrive
on the day of the concert!

On another occasion, Henriette had arranged to travel from
Paris 'to Berlin, as I promised a young composer to bring out
[introduce] his songs. A great responsibility as it depends so
much on how they are going to be reviewed'. Unfortunately
the recital 'had to be postponed for several months as I
caught a severe cold the last day in Paris'. Confined to 'an
hotel in Berlin with bronchitis', understandably anxious
about her voice, she consulted a specialist:

He advised a rest and I went to the famous 'Weisser
Hirsch' near Dresden, which was a unique place. In
winter you ran outside in a bathing suit in the snow,
then exercises and rest outside warmly packed in with
hot water bottles.

Prominently located on a steep hill overlooking a bend in
the river Elbe, the Weisser Hirsch (the White Stag) was
renowned for its air, light and hydrotherapies as well as
for the management of respiratory complaints. Established
by Dr Heinrich Lahmann in the 1880s, the famous health
resort continued to follow his ideas on naturopathic medi-
cine and the importance of diet, exercise and fresh air: air
baths and outdoor exercise, often in the nearby pine forest,
were among a number of treatments that implemented the

pioneering doctor's belief in the healing power of nature. So successful was this ethos that even before the Great War Weisser Hirsch had already grown into an extensive complex of villas, hotels and sanatoria.[17]

Over the years, Henriette gave a number of recitals, both at home and abroad, as a means of raising money for charitable causes. One of her more philanthropic ventures involved providing holidays for deprived children:

> In 1928 an Aunt of mine left me a villa on the sea front. We did not know the best way to use it. After talking it over with my friends we all came to the conclusion that I should give it for the use of children's summer holidays. We got a lot of donations; I gave a concert just for this occasion.

> We had to build a proper kitchen and shower room with a special floor and were able to have one hundred children each month but there was a lot of preparation for the upkeep of three hundred children. We had two nurses and a doctor to look after them, a cook and a few maids. The children arrived in dreadful condition; their clothes were immediately changed. It was a good cause and we had good results. After each month they gave a little performance and they benefited greatly. I attended these performances and they picked some flowers for a bouquet for me. It made me very happy to give such happiness to the poor children who had never had a holiday and they looked so well when they left.

The holidays which Henriette spent at her own villa in Jūrmala were among the happiest and most idyllic of times:

The summers were lovely. We went riding at 6 o'clock in the morning till 8 o'clock when the beach was empty. The golden sand was quite hard and one could canter like the wind. My daughter also took part and she became a good horsewoman. Then there was swimming in the sea, where the water was very clear. Tennis was also a great favourite and all these open-air activities were beneficial for my voice.

The routine allocation of separate hours for bathing and promenading was observed well into the 1930s,[18] as was the custom of nude bathing, a pursuit that invariably surprised foreign visitors. When Alfred Bossom, the Member of Parliament for Maidstone in Kent and President of the recently created Anglo-Baltic Society,[19] paid a visit to Latvia, 'He was very amused', Henriette recollected, 'about the bathing conditions at the Riga beach as there was nude bathing for men from eight to ten in the morning and from ten to twelve for women. Afterwards it was free for everybody'. In the afternoon, when the beach was open to both sexes, bathing suits were *de rigueur*; later in the day, many of the Riga seaside's female residents would appear in the loose-fitting beach pyjamas that were so fashionable in the 1930s.

Throughout the inter-war years Henriette travelled extensively in Europe: to England, to Italy, to France and to Germany, where her professional engagements gave her 'the opportunity to get to know the lovely German towns with the wonderful picture galleries and architecture. I was very interested in art and followed closely the Art Exhibitions, getting my first knowledge in Edinburgh as a student'. And when, just like her mother before her,

Tatiana was sent abroad to study, Henriette willingly put her career on hold: 'I could afford to miss a few months. She was seventeen and I had only spent the holidays with her. It was a good time to get to know her and to make her stay as pleasant as possible'. At the end of her first term, Henriette and Osip took Tatiana to Paris where they 'stayed at the Hotel Napoleon and awaited the New Year at the Opera House, which was always a brilliant affair: a ballet first and a supper afterwards'. The following Christmas they went to Switzerland, to St Moritz.

Then there were the visits to Europe's leading health resorts, whether in France or Germany, Czechoslovakia or Italy – 'In August my husband and I went to different spas and afterwards to Italy for a grapes' cure'. I have in front of me another photograph: it is 1937 and my grandparents are in Carlsbad (now Karlovy Vary). Smartly dressed (Henriette in a fitted suit, mid-calf length skirt pleated below the knees, small hat tilted at a fetching angle), they have no doubt come to take the waters and to walk through the woods which rise steeply above the town.

As ever, music remained central to Henriette's life:

I loved my songs and sometimes dreamed about them, especially Schubert's 'Der Wanderer an den Mond'. The wanderer goes from country to country, through mountains and woods, but he is never and nowhere at home, while the moon is everywhere at home and how happy the moon is to be in his own country everywhere. I used to get nightmares, losing my way and not finding my home anywhere. And, of course, one sings it like a dream.

165

Forced to lead a peripatetic life throughout the long years of war and revolution, I am tempted to ask whether it was in fact Henriette herself who was the wanderer.

CHAPTER 23

FINALE

The tone of Henriette's memoir suggests that, as far as she was concerned, the equilibrium and balance she now enjoyed were far preferable to the personal sacrifices she would have had to make in order to forge ahead with a potentially stellar European career. By the end of the 1930s, she had succeeded in resolving the inevitable conflict between career and family to her own satisfaction.

But the *modus vivendi* she had so painstakingly worked for would all too soon be shattered. In March 1938, Hitler invaded Austria. In the spring following the Anschluss, the German Führer turned his attention to the Sudetenland, the German-speaking region of Czechoslovakia.[1] In the middle of September, the British Prime Minster, Neville Chamberlain, flew to Germany, the first of three such trips he would undertake that autumn.[2] Hitler's demands were by now such that Chamberlain felt compelled to meet the German Chancellor face to face.

Towards the end of September, shortly after Chamberlain's second meeting with Hitler, Tatiana was preparing to go back to London where, with her mother's help, she had arranged to move into a small apartment:

We came by boat from Riga with antique drawing-room furniture, carpets, cutlery, a very nice dinner service – and everything necessary for two rooms; and there was a new wardrobe for Tania – evening dresses, fur coats, fur-lined coats and lots of other things.

There was one episode during the voyage to London when we reached the Kiel Canal and had to stop for twenty-four hours. It was 1938 and the Captain had to await instructions to continue the voyage in case of the outbreak of war.

When Henriette and Tatiana sailed out of Riga Harbour on 24 September 1938 the Sudeten Crisis was reaching a critical juncture. In London, the Government had already taken steps to implement the 'passive defence' of the civilian population; over the next few days 'protective trenches for use in air raids' would be dug 'in the Royal parks and at other open spaces',[3] gas masks would be issued and sand-bags supplied.

On 27 September, as Europe teetered on the brink of war, Chamberlain addressed the British people. Still intent on pursuing a policy of appeasement, he informed the nation that he was doing all he could to bring 'the present anxious and critical situation' to an end. That night, *The Times* went on to report, the Prime Minister had concluded his broadcast by assuring the 'men and women of Britain and the Empire' that he would 'work for peace to the last moment'.[4]

The following day, Chamberlain was invited to attend a hastily convened conference in Munich and the ship on which Henriette and Tatiana had been delayed was allowed to leave the Kiel Canal. However, despite the fact that 'Hitler had agreed to [temporarily] postpone either mobilization or military action against Czechoslovakia',[5] when

168

the two women docked in the Port of London they would have found that there had been no let-up in 'the progress of defensive preparations'[6] with 'Motor-vans equipped with loud-speakers' touring the streets 'urging laggards to collect their gas masks at once'.[7] Between 23 and 30 September, over thirty million gas masks would be issued, enough to protect the entire adult population.[8]

In the early hours of Friday 30 September, it was announced that Chamberlain had signed the Munich Agreement.[9] Later that day, the Prime Minister returned to London bringing 'peace with honour' and, as he famously informed the waiting crowds in Downing Street, 'I believe… it is peace for our time'.[10]

But although the crisis had been averted, the threat of war had by no means receded. Britain continued to prepare for a conflict that had begun to seem inevitable. In March 1939 Hitler occupied Prague, thereby breaking the Munich Agreement.[11] In July the Post Office was called on to deliver a number of Government-sponsored information leaflets. From air raid warnings to gas masks, from food supplies to lighting regulations, the public would be advised, *The Times* reported, as to the steps that were being taken to protect the civilian population. 'This does not mean that war is expected now, but it is everyone's duty to be prepared for the possibility of war'[12] was the uncompromising message that Tatiana would have received shortly before she left London in the middle of July.

Henriette would later look back to that last pre-war summer of 1939:

As usual Tania came home for the holiday. We went riding along the beach at six o'clock every morning, the sand was hard and one could canter without seeing a soul. We also did a lot of swimming. My husband used to go for a cure every year and I used to accompany him. This time he went earlier and I stayed with Tania at the seaside. In the middle of August we went to Libau [Liepāja] to visit my father. [Henriette's mother had died in 1931]. We stayed there for a few days and then went back home.

They arrived in Dzintari just in time to hear the disconcerting news that Germany and the Soviet Union had reached agreement on a non-aggression pact. Events moved remarkably swiftly. On Wednesday 23 August, the German Foreign Minister, Joachim von Ribbentrop, flew to Moscow for talks with his counterpart, the Soviet Foreign Minister, Vyacheslav Molotov. The following morning, Thursday 24 August, it was announced that the two countries had signed the pact.

The news was greeted with consternation. *The Times* informed its readers that it had 'reliably, though unofficially, learned' that Poland would probably be divided between Germany and Russia, with 'Germany to obtain Danzig, the Corridor and Polish Western Silesia'.[13] The newspaper was also quick to recognise the concerns of 'the countries in the immediate danger zone' such as 'the three small Baltic states', who 'fear they may become once more a battleground, or, worse still, an object for division into spheres of influence between Slav and Teuton'.[14] And indeed, although the pact had ostensibly been confined to the issue of co-operation, it was also secretly intended to divide eastern Europe between Germany and the Soviet Union.

The conclusion of the German-Soviet agreement convinced Tatiana that she should return to London earlier than she had previously intended. She encouraged her mother to accompany her. 'I did not want to go', Henriette admitted, 'but Tania persuaded me it would be just for a short time'. Understandably concerned that it might be inadvisable to travel through the Polish Corridor:

> We thought to go back via Sweden. When we phoned the Swedish Embassy, they told us that they weren't issuing any more visas. That gave us rather a shock and my daughter insisted that we should leave the next morning for London.

Henriette and Tatiana resolved to set out immediately. On the evening of Thursday 24 August, they took a local train from the Riga seaside to the Latvian capital: 'We left our villa by night and the cook even managed to fry us a chicken for the journey'. A small, inconsequential memory; they had in fact deliberately 'left everything behind'. Years later, Henriette could still picture the pearl earrings she habitually wore, lying casually on her bedroom windowsill, awaiting her return.

Later that night, they telephoned some friends:

> ...who advised us just to take small suitcases which we could carry ourselves as one did not know how the trains would work. We phoned our dressmaker and collected some clothes that were with her and got ready for the train. They did not issue any sleepers but we got some tickets to London. We did not take any money or jewellery in case there was a search on the train.

171

On Friday 25 August, Henriette and Tatiana boarded 'the morning train to Berlin'. I still have my mother's old Latvian passport, with its patchwork of stamps, which has enabled me to chart their journey across Europe:

Joniskis 1939 VIII. 25
Near the Latvian-Lithuanian border

Eydtkuhnen-Bahnhof 25. AUG. 1939

The East Prussian frontier station of Eydtkuhnen was located just over the border from Lithuania. It was from here that they would have taken the train for Berlin, travelling through the Polish Corridor, the land route that had been created after the Great War in order to give Poland access to the Baltic Sea – an arrangement that had effectively cut German East Prussia off from the rest of Germany. Henriette remembered how 'During the journey through the Polish Corridor there were a lot of German soldiers telling us that when we came back it would all be German'. Less than a week later, on Friday 1 September 1939, Germany did indeed invade Poland.

More disturbing for me is the knowledge that Hitler had originally intended to invade Poland on 26 August. Only two weeks earlier, on 12 August, from his mountain retreat at Obersalzberg in the Bavarian Alps, the German Führer had given detailed instructions for the proposed invasion.[15] These orders were only countermanded at the eleventh hour: at 7.45 p.m. on the evening of the 25 August Hitler called off the attack on Poland, an attack that had been due to begin at precisely 4.30 a.m. the following morning.[16]

172

When they reached the German capital, Henriette was surprised to find that, 'In Berlin there were big crowds of people leaving the country, there were also quite a lot of English people. We did not know anything about all this'. She would no doubt have been unaware that, following the announcement of the Molotov-Ribbentrop Pact, on 24 August the British Embassy had advised 'British residents...to leave Germany. The message', the *Times* correspondent reported that day, 'which "strongly advised them to consider urgently" the temporary removal of their residence from Germany was not signed by the Ambassador, but has been taken throughout the comparatively small British colony in Berlin and elsewhere as a fully official warning. British residents are, therefore, leaving to-night so far as possible, including journalists'.[17]

From Berlin, they travelled west across Germany. Spandau, Stendal, Hanover, Osnabrück, the stations flashed past as they made their way towards the Dutch frontier:

In the train from Berlin to the frontier there were several German officers asking to see our passports. Some German couples were taken off the train; they had missed their time of leaving, as they could not decide to leave their country. There was a little girl brought by her grandmother and put in our compart-ment. She asked us to look after her until we got to London, where her parents would meet her.

Bentheim ausgereist 26.8.39
The German customs post

DOORLAATPOST OLDENZAAL 26 AUG. 1939
The Dutch checkpoint

They had left Germany. They had got through. Then the cross-channel ferry from the Hook of Holland and the final stamp:

IMMIGRATION OFFICER HARWICH 26 AUG 1939

Although the cross-channel ferries continued to run as people hurriedly fled Continental Europe, by 1 September the Harwich-Zeebrugge passenger service had 'been suspended';[18] 'sailings from Harwich to the Hook of Holland and from Harwich to Antwerp' would be cancelled the following day.[19]

Such was the confusion that, less than two days after Henriette and Tatiana crossed the German frontier, reports were reaching London that 'all railway traffic to and from Germany' would be 'stopped' on Monday 28 August.[20] If this had in fact been true, they would have made it with only a day to spare.

The two women arrived in London in the early hours of 27 August. They went straight to Tatiana's flat from where, Henriette recalled:

We tried to phone to Paris and get into touch with my husband. We phoned the hotel where he usually stayed and there he was. We begged him to come to England immediately as there will be war announced quite soon. He told us that he had to go back to Riga as he had very important documents of his clients in his safe and that he must save them.

On Sunday 27 August, the Central War Room in Whitehall was ready for action;[21] in London, sandbags were filled and stacked up in front of buildings.[22] On Friday 1 September, the first night of the blackout, the city was plunged into unaccustomed darkness.[23] Two days later, Londoners, who had just been informed by Neville Chamberlain that Britain was at war with Germany, were dismayed to hear, only minutes after the Prime Minister had concluded his momentous broadcast, the ominous wail of the air raid sirens[24] – a false alarm that was followed shortly afterwards by the welcome sound of the 'All Clear'.[25]

On Sunday 3 September 1939, Henriette understood that once again her life had changed forever: 'It was a great shock when war was declared on the Sunday and I knew that for the second time in my life I had lost all my possessions: houses, money, jewellery and the whole of my comfortable life'.

By the end of the war, she would also have lost her husband, her family, her career and her country.

CHAPTER 24

EPILOGUE

Henriette and Osip never spoke again. Osip did return to Riga after undertaking a 'perilous journey through Sweden'. For a time my grandparents exchanged letters: 'We got a few letters at the beginning of the war, very short ones', Henriette remembered, 'as everything was censored'.

From the relative safety of wartime England, Tatiana later observed: 'The Russo-German Treaty of the 23rd of August 1939 came as an unexpected and terrible blow to us. Lying between Russia and Germany it became clear to all of us that we would from now on be at the absolute mercy of these two countries and exposed to any form of aggression they might choose... We decided to retain our attitude of strict neutrality but, from that day in August on, there was tragedy in the air of our countries and a feeling that everybody was slowly bowing to some inevitable fate. A secret clause concerning the Baltic states was probably attached to the Russo-German Non Aggression Pact, but we did not yet know from which side our fate would come: Germany or Russia?'

The Molotov-Ribbentrop Pact had in fact secretly transferred Latvia to the Soviet sphere of domination.

In the autumn of 1939, the Latvian Foreign Minister was summoned to Moscow. On 5 October he signed a Pact of Mutual Assistance with the Soviet Union. The terms of the agreement clearly stated that the continuing independence of the Latvian Republic, and ostensibly the safety of the Soviet Union, would depend on the USSR being permitted to lease airfields and naval bases in Liepāja (Libava) and Ventspils (Vindava) for a 'reasonable' rent.[1] The Latvian Government had effectively been forced to allow the Soviets to establish military bases on their territory. As Tatiana remarked, 'This was the first step'.

In June 1940, despite Russian assurances that Latvia's sovereignty would be respected, the Red Army invaded the Baltic states. Less than two months later Latvia had been incorporated into the Soviet Union. A communist regime was implemented: Stalinist purges were conducted, and numerous Latvian citizens were imprisoned. The following year thousands more would be deported to Siberia.

Henriette lost all contact with her family:

We got the news that my father had been arrested. He was an estate owner and a capitalist and he had very bad treatment from the Russians; they imprisoned him and we don't know how he died. That was a terrible blow to me and it shook me terribly.

We also got one last letter from my husband asking us to return to Riga, as the Russians offered me a professorship at the conservatoire. We showed this letter to Professor Brierly [Professor of Public International Law at Oxford University] and he said one could see that my husband had been made to write this letter, as he could not want us to return and we should ignore it. Then all news stopped.

On 22 June 1941 Nazi Germany invaded the Soviet Union. Latvia was overrun: by 7 July the German army had occupied the whole country. Martial law was enforced and the Holocaust with all its horrors and atrocities was unleashed.[2]

At the end of the Second World War, the pendulum would swing the other way; when Russia resumed her domination of the Baltic states, the Soviet Socialist Republic of Latvia once again became part of the USSR. The Iron Curtain had descended.

In England, Henriette had made her own contribution to the war effort by singing for 'different charitable institutions' and, when Churchill and Stalin had united against a common enemy, she had willingly given concerts in aid of Mrs Churchill's Red Cross Aid to Russia Fund:

> There was a cellist, a very fine pianist, and myself. We travelled to all sorts of remote places. I shall never forget one of our concerts in a village where we performed in a school. They had never seen a singer, especially in evening dress. There was great excitement. The parson and his wife invited me to lunch the next day and they could not get over the treat they had had. It was quite fun and took the gloom away.

She never sang professionally again. For Henriette, her own survival would always be tempered by the losses she had suffered: the husband, the father, the brother and sister who had predeceased her. And when it came to the career for which she had worked so hard, a few telling words jotted down inside the back cover of her notebook – 'the unfulfilled, the broken hopes'; 'the lost opportunities' – reveal the extent to which her life had once again been shaped and deflected by the vagaries of history, by the tumultuous historical events over which she had never had any control.

Henriette died in 1979. She had lived in England for forty years. Devoted to her daughter Tatiana, her granddaughters and her great-grandsons, her resilient nature had enabled her to make a new life for herself. Her indomitable spirit had not deserted her.

Acknowledgements

With so much of Henriette's life dominated by political upheaval, it is perhaps fitting that it was the fall of the Iron Curtain, another defining historical event, that led me to revisit her memoir and allowed me to embark on what has proved to be a truly fascinating journey. And so, my deepest thanks must inevitably go to my grandmother because, after all, without her words, without her memories, this book would not exist.

I could not have written *Baltic Sumers, Russian Winter* without the assistance of a number of individuals and institutions, in particular, the enormously helpful staff at the London Library. In addition, the London Library, the British Library and the National Archives at Kew have furnished me with invaluable material.

I should also like to thank Georgina Aldridge; Richard Augustus; Russian cultural historian Rosamund Bartlett for allowing me to quote from her work; Nicola Beauman at Persephone Books for giving me permission to quote from Christine Longford's *Making Conversation* (Persephone Book no. 83); Grant Buttars for giving me access to and allowing me to reproduce extracts from the Masson Hall Archive at the University of Edinburgh; Antony Bye for giving me permission to quote from *The Musical Times*; Sarah Elizabeth Gundlach at the Louisiana State Museum Historical Center

181

Archives; Christina Hardyment, Senior Executor of the Arthur Ransome Literary Estate, for allowing me to quote from Arthur Ransome's *Six Weeks in Russia in 1919*; Rik Hendriks at the Nederlands Musiek Instituut; Rita Krūmina and Agita Leja at the Liepāja Museum; Elly Pace; Pen and Sword Books, Frontline Books, for permission to quote from R. H. Bruce Lockhart's *Memoirs of a British Agent*; F + W Media International for allowing me to quote from *Baedeker's Russia 1914*; the Russianist Harvey Pitcher for giving me permission to quote from *Chekhov's Leading Lady: A Portrait of the Actress Olga Knipper* and from *Muir & Mirrielees: The Scottish Partnership that Became a Household Name in Russia*; Patricia Roach; Jane Simmonds; John Sutherland for allowing me to reproduce an extract from the *Edinburgh University Journal*, and for kindly sending me other material relating to Professor Gerard Baldwin Brown; *The Times* News Syndication for allowing me to use extracts from contemporary editions of the newspaper; the *Times-Picayune*; Ilze Voitina at The Latvian Embassy in London for her assistance.

While it is impossible to thank everyone who has helped me to bring this book to fruition, I would particularly like to thank the many friends and relations who have unfailingly encouraged me over the last ten years as I continued to explore the background to Henriette's life.

I owe an enormous debt of gratitude to my family: to my sons James and Charles (Henriette's great-grandsons), who even now remember her with affection; to my husband David, endlessly supportive and a resourceful and stimulating travelling companion; above all, I should like to thank my sister Eleonor (Henriette's other granddaughter) without whose advice, encouragement and enthusiasm I would never have finished this book.

Photographic Acknowledgements

Back cover: Kremlin, Moscow, c.1910 (Photo: akg-images/ Krasnogorsk, Film Archive).

Tsar Nicholas II and the Tsarina, Libau, 23 August 1903 (Liepāja Museum, photo LM4171).

Grosse Strasse, Libau, beginning of the twentieth century (Liepāja Museum, photo LM 18658).

Kurhaus, Libau, c.1900 (Liepāja Museum, photo LM22960).

Bade Strasse, Libau, beginning of the twentieth century (Liepāja Museum, photo LMzp 2039).

Frances Helen Simson outside the House of Lords, 1908 (Edinburgh University Special Collections).

Suffrage procession, Princes Street, Edinburgh, October 1909 (City of Edinburgh Museums and Galleries).

Feodor Ivanovich Chaliapin in the role of Boris Godunov, 1913 (De Agostini Picture Library/G. Dagli Orti/Bridgeman Images).

Russian Revolution, Moscow, 1917. Barricade on Arbat Square, 2 November (OS) (Photo: akg-images).

Red Army soldiers entering Riga, 3 January 1919 (Photo: akg-images/ Sputnik).

All other photographs are from family collections.

Every effort has been made to trace copyright-holders. The publisher will be happy to make good in future editions any errors or omissions brought to their attention.

Notes

Chapter 2: Overture

1 *The Times*, Sep 04, 1903.

2 *Ibid.* Sep 01, 1903.

Chapter 3: Libau

1 Gintners, Jānis, *Liepājas gadsimti* (Liepāja, Liepājas Muzejs, 2004).

2 *Pastaigas Liepājā: Pilsētas 370 Gadu Jubilejā* (Liepāja, Kaste, 1995).

3 Figes, Orlando. *A people's tragedy: the Russian Revolution, 1891–1924* (London, Cape, 1996), p. 57.

4 Official history (naval and military) of the Russo-Japanese war (London, H. M. Stationery Office, 1920).

5 *British documents on the origins of the War, 1898–1914,* edited by G. P. Gooch and Harold Temperley (London, H. M. Stationery Office, 1929), vol. IV, p. 84.

6 Figes, Orlando. *A people's tragedy: the Russian Revolution, 1891–1924* (London, Cape, 1996), pp. 173–178.

7 *The Times*, Jan 23, 1905.

8 Kaun, Alexander Samuel. *Maxim Gorky and his Russia* (London, Jonathan Cape, 1932), p. 355.

9 *The Blackwell encyclopaedia of the Russian Revolution*, edited by Harold Shukman (Oxford, Blackwell Reference, 1988).

10 Figes, Orlando. *A people's tragedy: the Russian Revolution, 1891–1924* (London, Cape, 1996), p. 185; Bilmanis, Alfred. *A History of Latvia* (Princeton, NJ, Princeton University Press, 1951), p. 264.

185

11 Bilmanis, Alfred. *A History of Latvia* (Princeton, NJ, Princeton University Press, 1951), p. 265.

12 Raun, Toivo U. 'The Revolution of 1905 in the Baltic Provinces and Finland'. *Slavic Review*, vol. 43, no. 3, 1984, pp. 453–467, JSTOR; Williams, Robert C. 'Russians in Germany: 1900–1914'. *Journal of Contemporary History*, vol. 1. no. 4, 1966, p. 143, JSTOR; Plakans, Andrejs. *Historical Dictionary of Latvia*, 2nd ed. (Lanham, MD, Scarecrow Press, 2008), pp. 218–220.

13 Figes, Orlando. *A people's tragedy: the Russian Revolution, 1891–1924* (London, Cape, 1996), p. 192.

Chapter 5: Edinburgh

1 Robinson, Jane. *Bluestockings: the remarkable story of the first women to fight for an education* (London, Penguin Books, 2010), p. 54.

2 Gordon, Peter and Doughan, David. *Dictionary of British women's organisations, 1825–1960* (London, Woburn Press, 2001).

3 Masson Hall Archives EUA GD58, the University of Edinburgh.

4 Ibid.

5 Ibid.

6 Ibid.

7 Ibid.

8 Longford, Christine. *Making conversation* (London, Persephone Books, 2009), p. 148.

9 *Baedeker's Russia 1914* by Karl Baedeker, David & Charles/George Allen & Unwin, 1971, p. xxi.

10 Masson Hall archives EUA GD58, the University of Edinburgh.

11 Ibid.

12 Crawford, Elizabeth. *The women's suffrage movement: a reference guide, 1866–1928* (London, UCL Press/Taylor and Francis Group, 1999), pp. 363–364.

13 Representation of the People (Scotland) Act 1868. legislation. gov.uk.

14 House of Lords Law Report. *The Times*, Dec 11, 1908.

15 Longford, Christine. *Making conversation* (London, Persephone Books, 2009), p. 176.

16 Ibid. p. 180.

17 *University of Edinburgh Journal*, Summer Number 1930, vol. III, p. 218.

18 Reid, Louis Arnaud. *Yesterdays today: a journey into philosophy*, edited by Nicholas Reid (Canberra, Samizdat Press, 2013), p. 57.

19 McBriar, A. M. *Fabian socialism and English politics, 1884–1918* (London, Cambridge University Press, 1962), pp. 165–169.

20 metoffice.gov.uk.

21 *The Times*, Oct 11, 1909.

Chapter 6: Frankfurt

1 Cahn, Peter. 'Frankfurt'. *Grove Music Online. Oxford Music Online.* Oxford University Press.

2 Reich, Nancy B. 'Schumann, Clara'. *Grove Music Online. Oxford Music Online.* Oxford University Press.

3 *The Musical Times*, October 1910.

4 Pascall, Robert. 'Knorr, Iwan'. *Grove Music Online. Oxford Music Online.* Oxford University Press.

5 Haward, Lawrence W. and Ring, Reinhard. 'Jaques-Dalcroze, Emile'. *Grove Music Online. Oxford Music Online.* Oxford University Press.

6 Pascall, Robert. 'Stockhausen'. *Grove Music Online. Oxford Music Online.* Oxford University Press.

7 Bowen, José A., et al. 'Mengelberg'. *Grove Music Online. Oxford Music Online.* Oxford University Press.

8 *The Musical Times*, December 1912.

9 *Ibid.* 1912.

10 McVeagh, Diana. 'Elgar, Sir Edward'. *Grove Music Online. Oxford Music Online.* Oxford University Press.

11 Blumo, Mary. *Côte d'Azur: inventing the French Riviera* (London, Thames and Hudson, 1992), p. 64.

12 Bartlett, Rosamund. *Chekhov: scenes from a life* (London, Free Press, 2004), p. 248.

13 Borovsky, Victor. *Chaliapin: a critical biography* (London, Hamish Hamilton, 1988), p. 377.

14 Diaghilev Ballets Russes in Monte Carlo in April 1911. *Överdådets konst II, The Art of Extravagance II: Kostymer från Diaghilevs Ryska Baletten I Paris* (Dansmuseet Stockholm, 2004).

15 Baedeker, Karl. *Le Sud-Est de la France du Jura à la Méditerranée y Compris la Corse* (Leipzig, Karl Baedeker, 1910), p. 452.

Chapter 7: Riga

1 Plakans, Andrejs. *Historical Dictionary of Latvia*, 2nd ed. (Lanham, MD, Scarecrow Press, 2008).

2 Dollinger, Philippe. *The German Hansa*, translated and edited by D. S. Ault and S. H. Steinberg (London, Macmillan, 1970).

3 Kennard, Howard Percy and Heyking, A. Baron, *The Russian Year-Book for 1911* (London, Eyre and Spottiswoode, Ltd., 1911), p. 239.

4 Bowman, Linda. 'Russia's First Income Taxes: The Effects of Modernized Taxes on Commerce and Industry, 1885–1914'. *Slavic Review*, vol. 52, no. 2, 1993, pp. 256–282 and note p. 262, JSTOR.

5 Lodijensky, N. 'The Forests of Russia'. *Russia: its industries and trade/Issued by order of State Secretary S. J. de Witte…minister of finance* (Russia, Ministerstvo finansov; Glasgow, 1901), p. 322.

6 *Latvia as a transit country Western Europe – Russia: Latvian ports and railways. [b.v.]: [b.i.], 1923*, p. 4.

7 *Ibid.* p. 4.

8 *Baedeker's Russia 1914* by Karl Baedeker, David & Charles/George Allen & Unwin, 1971, p. 60.

9 *Ibid.* p. 54.

10 Henriksson, Anders. 'Riga', in Hamm, Michael F. (ed.), *The City in late imperial Russia* (Bloomington, IN, Indiana University Press, 1986), pp. 177–189.

11 Wood, Ruth Kedzie. *The tourist's Russia* (London, Andrew Melrose, 1912), p. 58.

12 Kolbergs, Andris. *The story of Riga* (Riga, Jāņa Sēta, 1999), p. 104.

13 Grosa, Silvija. *Art Nouveau in Riga* (Riga, Jumava), p. 3.

14 Sollohub, Edith. *The Russian Countess: escaping revolutionary Russia* (Exeter, Impress Books, 2009).

15 *Baedeker's Russia 1914* by Karl Baedeker, David & Charles/George Allen & Unwin, 1971, p. 63.

16 Wood, Ruth Kedzie. *The tourist's Russia* (London, Andrew Melrose, 1912), pp. 59–60.

17 *Baedeker's Russia 1914* by Karl Baedeker, David & Charles/George Allen & Unwin, 1971, p. 63.

18 *Jūrmala: nature and cultural heritage,* editor Laima Slava (Riga, Neptuns, *c.*2004), pp. 212–213.

Chapter 8: St Petersburg

1 *The Times,* Jun 24, 1913.

2 Dowler, Wayne. *Russia in 1913* (DeKalb, IL, Northern Illinois University Press, 2010), p. 6.

3 *The Times,* Mar 07, 1913.

4 *Ibid.*

5 Figes, Orlando. *A people's tragedy: the Russian Revolution, 1891–1924* (London, Jonathan Cape, 1996), pp. 3–6.

6 *The Times,* Mar 07, 1913.

7 Buchanan, George, Sir. *My mission to Russia and other diplomatic memories* (London, Cassell and Company Ltd, 1923), vol. I., p. 173.

8 Figes, Orlando. *A people's tragedy: the Russian Revolution, 1891–1924* (London, Cape, 1996), p. 13.

9 Dowler, Wayne. *Russia in 1913* (DeKalb, IL, Northern Illinois University Press, 2010), p. 77.

10 Figes, Orlando. *A people's tragedy: the Russian Revolution, 1891–1924* (London, Cape, 1996), p. 232.

11 Bradshaw, George. *Bradshaw's Continental Railway Guide 1913* (Oxford, Old House books, 2012 [London, Henry Blacklock & Co, 1913]), pp. 1029–1030.

12 Williams, Harold. *Russia of the Russians* (London, Pitman & Sons, 1914), p. 417.

13 *Baedeker's Russia 1914* by Karl Baedeker, David & Charles/George Allen & Unwin, 1971, p. 274.

14 Fleming, John and Honour, Hugh. *The Penguin dictionary of decorative arts* (London, Penguin Books, 1979).

15 Bainbridge, Henry Charles. *Peter Carl Fabergé, goldsmith and jeweller to the Russian imperial court: his life and work*, with a foreword by Sacheverell Sitwell (London, Spring Books, 1966).

16 Brumfield, William C. *A history of Russian architecture*, text and photographs by William Craft Brumfield (Cambridge, Cambridge University Press, 1993), pp. 453–454.

17 Bainbridge, Henry Charles. *Peter Carl Fabergé, goldsmith and jeweller to the Russian imperial court: his life and work*, with a foreword by Sacheverell Sitwell (London, Spring Books, 1966).

18 *Ibid.*

19 Fleming, John and Honour, Hugh. *The Penguin dictionary of decorative arts* (London, Penguin Books, 1979).

20 Wortman, Richard. *Scenarios of power: myth and ceremony in Russian monarchy* (Princeton, NJ; Chichester, Princeton University Press, 2000), vol. II, p. 510.

Chapter 9: War

1 Figes, Orlando. *A people's tragedy: the Russian Revolution, 1891–1924* (London, Cape, 1996), p. 232.

2 *The Times*, Jul 20–25, 1914.

3 *Ibid.* Jul 24, 1914.

4 Salmon, Patrick. *Scandinavia and the great powers 1890–1940* (Cambridge, Cambridge University Press, 2002), p. 123.

5 *The Times*, Jul 15, 1914.

6 metoffice.gov.uk.

7 *The Times*, Jul 20, 1914.

8 *Ibid.*

9 *Ibid.*

10 *Ibid.*

11 *Ibid.* Jul 25, 1914.

12 Salmon, Patrick. *Scandinavia and the great powers 1890–1940* (Cambridge, Cambridge University Press, 2002), p. 123.

13 Peacock, Netta. *The Russian Year-Book for 1915* (London, Eyre and Spottiswoode, Ltd., 1915); Hurd, Archibald. 'The Fleets of our Allies', *The Quarterly Review* (London, John Murray, 1917).

14 Stone, Norman. *The eastern front, 1914–1917* (London, Hodder and Stoughton, 1975), pp. 44–69.

15 Figes, Orlando. *A people's tragedy: the Russian Revolution, 1891–1924* (London, Cape, 1996), p. 256.

16 Washburn, Stanley. *The Russian campaign: April to August, 1915* (London, Andrew Melrose Ltd., 1915), p. 69.

17 *The Times*, May 12, 1915.

18 Sondhaus, Lawrence. *The Great War at sea: a naval history of the First World War* (Cambridge, Cambridge University Press, 2014), p. 195.

19 Plakans, Andrejs. *Historical Dictionary of Latvia*, 2nd ed. (Lanham, MD, Scarecrow Press, 2008), p. 272.

20 Urch, Reginald Oliver Gilling. *We generally shoot Englishmen* (London, George Allen & Unwin, 1936), p. 20.

21 Sanborn, Joshua A. *Imperial apocalypse: the great war and the destruction of the Russian empire* (Oxford, Oxford University Press, 2014), p. 85.

22 *The Times*, Aug 06, 1915.

Chapter 10: An Estate in the Country

1 Stone, Norman. *The eastern front, 1914–1917* (London, Hodder and Stoughton, 1975), p. 182.

2 Gatrell, Peter. *Russia's First World War: a social and economic history* (Harlow, Pearson/Longman, 2005).

3 Lodijensky, N. 'The Forests of Russia'. *Russia: its industries and trade/Issued by order of State Secretary S. J. de Witte…minister of finance* (Russia, Ministerstvo finansov; Glasgow, Hay Nisbet, 1901), p. 322.

4 *Ibid.* p. 321.

5 Westwood, J. N. *A history of Russian railways* (London, Allen & Unwin, 1964), p. 134.

6 Solzhenitsyn, Alexander. *August 1914*, translated by Michael Glenny (London, The Bodley Head Ltd, 1972), p. 71.

Chapter 11: Moscow

1 Colton, Timothy J. *Moscow: governing the socialist metropolis* (Cambridge, MA, Belknap Press of Harvard University Press, 1995), p. 44.

2 Bunin, Ivan. *Cursed days: a diary of Revolution*, translated from the Russian, with an introduction and notes by Thomas Gaiton Marullo (Chicago, IL, Ivan R. Dee, 1998), footnote, p. 49.

3 Colton, Timothy J. *Moscow: governing the socialist metropolis* (Cambridge, MA, Belknap Press of Harvard University Press, 1995), p. 46.

4 *Ibid.* p. 41.

5 *The Times*, Jun 01, 1908.

6 Bartlett, Rosamund. 'Russian culture: 1801–1917', in Perrie, Maureen, Lieven, Dominic and Suny, Ronald Grigor (eds.), *The Cambridge history of Russia* (Cambridge, Cambridge University Press, 2006), vol. II, p. 107.

7 *Ibid.* pp. 108–109.

8 *Ibid.* p. 115.

9 *Ibid.* p. 108.

10 Worrall, Nick. *The Moscow Art Theatre* (London, Routledge, 1996).

11 Bartlett, Rosamund. 'Russian culture: 1801–1917', in Perrie, Maureen, Lieven, Dominic and Suny, Ronald Grigor (eds.), *The Cambridge history of Russia* (Cambridge, Cambridge University Press, 2006), vol. II, p. 109.

12 Stanislavsky, Constantin. *My Life in Art*, translated from the Russian by J. J. Robbins (London, Geoffrey Bles, 1924), pp. 388.

13 Worrall, Nick. *The Moscow Art Theatre* (London, Routledge, 1996), p. 73.

14 Stanislavsky, Constantin. *My Life in Art*, translated from the Russian by J. J. Robbins (London, Geoffrey Bles, 1924), pp. 388–389.

15 Pitcher, Harvey J. *Chekhov's leading lady: a portrait of the actress Olga Knipper* (London, John Murray, 1979), p. 29.

16 Bartlett, Rosamund. 'Russian culture: 1801–1917', in Perrie, Maureen, Lieven, Dominic and Suny, Ronald Grigor (eds.), *The Cambridge history of Russia* (Cambridge, Cambridge University Press, 2006), vol. II, p. 110.

17 Pitcher, Harvey J. *Chekhov's leading lady: a portrait of the actress Olga Knipper* (London, John Murray, 1979), p. 191.

18 *Ibid.* p. 24.

19 *Ibid.* p. 94.

20 *Ibid.* p. 177.

21 *Ibid.* p. 193.

22 *Ibid.* pp. 193–194.

23 *Ibid.* p. 177.

24 Sayler, Oliver Martin. *The Russian Theatre* (New York, Brentano's Publishers, 1922).

25 Pitcher, Harvey J. *Chekhov's leading lady: a portrait of the actress Olga Knipper* (London, John Murray, 1979), p. 214.

26 Worrall, Nick. *The Moscow Art Theatre* (London, Routledge, 1996), p. 82.

27 *The Musical Times*, November 1915.

28 Radó, Sándor. *Guide-book to the Soviet Union*, compiled by A. Radó, issued by the Society for cultural relations of the Soviet Union with Foreign Countries (New York, International Publishers Co., 1928).

29 Kotkin, Stephen. *Stalin* (London, Allen Lane, an imprint of Penguin Books, 2014), note p. 808.

30 *Baedeker's Russia 1914* by Karl Baedeker, David & Charles/George Allen & Unwin, 1971, p. 301.

31 Colton, Timothy J. *Moscow: governing the socialist metropolis* (Cambridge, MA, Belknap Press of Harvard University Press, 1995), p. 40.

32 Pitcher, Harvey J. *Muir & Mirrielees: the Scottish partnership that became a household name in Russia* (Cromer, Swallow House Books, 1994).

33 *Ibid*. p. 164.

34 *Ibid*. p. 160.

35 *Baedeker's Russia 1914* by Karl Baedeker, David & Charles/George Allen & Unwin, 1971, p. 274.

36 Pitcher, Harvey J. *Muir & Mirrielees: the Scottish partnership that became a household name in Russia* (Cromer, Swallow House Books, 1994), p. 173.

37 *Baedeker's Russia 1914* by Karl Baedeker, David & Charles/George Allen & Unwin, 1971, p. 299.

38 *Ibid*.

39 *Ibid*. p. 274.

40 Polonsky, Rachel. *Molotov's magic lantern: a journey in Russian history* (London, Faber and Faber, 2010), p. 23.

Chapter 12: Chaliapin

1 *Baedeker's Russia 1914* by Karl Baedeker, David & Charles/George Allen & Unwin, 1971, p. xxi.

2 Ely, Christopher. 'The Origins of Russian Scenery: Volga River Tourism and Russian Landscape Aesthetics'. *Slavic Review*, vol. 62, no. 4, 2003, pp. 666–682, JSTOR.

3 Troyat, Henri. *La vie quotidienne en Russie au temps du dernier tsar* (Paris, Hachette, 1959), p. 307.

4 Hubback, J. H. *Russian realities: being impressions gathered during some recent journeys in Russia* (London, John Lane, 1915), p. 192.

5 *Baedeker's Russia 1914* by Karl Baedeker, David & Charles/George Allen & Unwin, 1971, p. 348.

6 Nikulin, Lev. 'Chaliapin: a reminiscence', in Chaliapin, Fyodor Ivanovich, Gorky, Maksim, Froud, Nina and Hanley, James, *Chaliapin: an autobiography as told to Maxim Gorky*, with supplementary correspondence and notes, compiled and edited by Nina Froud and James Hanley (London, Macdonald, 1968), p. 297.

7 Chaliapine, Fedor and Pierre, André. *Ma vie*, traduit du Russe par André Pierre (Paris, Albin Michel, 1932), p. 91.

8 *Ibid.* p. 97.

9 *Ibid.* pp. 97–98.

10 *Ibid.* pp. 93–94.

11 Gorky, Maksim, Barratt, Andrew and Scherr, Barry. *Maksim Gorky: selected letters*, selected, translated, and edited by Andrew Barratt and Barry P. Scherr (Oxford, Clarendon Press, 1997), note, p. 190.

12 Borovsky, Victor. *Chaliapin: a critical biography* (London, Hamish Hamilton, 1988), pp. 359–362.

13 *Ibid.* p. 240.

14 Bartlett, Rosamund. 'Russian culture: 1801–1917', in Perrie, Maureen, Lieven, Dominic and Suny, Ronald Grigor (eds.), *The*

Cambridge history of Russia (Cambridge, Cambridge University Press, 2006), vol. II, p. 112.

15 Borovsky, Victor. *Chaliapin: a critical biography* (London, Hamish Hamilton, 1988), p. 319.

16 Alexander Golovin. Portrait of *Feodor Ivanovich Chaliapin in the role of Boris Godunov*, 1912. State Russian Museum, St Petersburg. *From Russia: French and Russian Master Paintings 1870–1925 from Moscow and St Petersburg*, catalogue by Natalia Ardashnikova et al. (London, Royal Academy of Arts, 2008), p. 227.

17 Nikolai Kharitonov. *Chaliapin as Boris Godunov, 1916*. State Central A. A. Bakhrushin Theatre Museum, Moscow.

18 Chaliapine, Fedor and Pierre, André. *Ma vie*, traduit du Russe par André Pierre (Paris, Albin Michel, 1932), p. 109.

19 *The Times*, Jun 06, 1914.

20 Borovsky, Victor. *Chaliapin: a critical biography* (London, Hamish Hamilton, 1988), pp. 33–53; Chaliapin, Fyodor Ivanovich, Gorky, Maksim, Froud, Nina and Hanley, James. *Chaliapin: an autobiography as told to Maxim Gorky*, with supplementary correspondence and notes, compiled and edited by Nina Froud and James Hanley (London, Macdonald, 1968), p. 121.

21 *Baedeker's Russia 1914* by Karl Baedeker, David & Charles/George Allen & Unwin, 1971, p. 461.

22 Chaliapin, Fyodor Ivanovich, Gorky, Maksim, Froud, Nina and Hanley, James. *Chaliapin: an autobiography as told to Maxim Gorky*, with supplementary correspondence and notes, compiled and edited by Nina Froud and James Hanley (London, Macdonald, 1968), pp. 212–213.

23 *Baedeker's Russia 1914* by Karl Baedeker, David & Charles/George Allen & Unwin, 1971, p. 348.

24 *Ibid*.

25 Chamberlain, Lesley. *Volga, Volga: a journey down Russia's great river* (London, Picador, 1995), p. 63.

26 *Baedeker's Russia 1914* by Karl Baedeker, David & Charles/George Allen & Unwin, 1971, p. 433.

27 Hubback, J. H. *Russian realities: being impressions gathered during some recent journeys in Russia* (London, John Lane, 1915), p. 211.

28 *Ibid.* pp. 210–211.

29 *Baedeker's Russia 1914* by Karl Baedeker, David & Charles/George Allen & Unwin, 1971, p. 347.

30 Ross, Edward Alsworth. *Russia in upheaval* (New York, The Century Company, 1918 [London, T. Fisher Unwin, 1919]), p. 42.

Chapter 13: A House in the Country

1 Browder, Robert Paul and Kerensky, Alexander. *The Russian Provisional Government, 1917: documents*, selected and edited by Robert Paul Browder and Alexander F. Kerensky (Stanford, CA, Stanford University Press, 1961), vol. II, pp. 526–527.

2 Roosevelt, Priscilla. *Life on the Russian country estate: a social and cultural history* (New Haven, CT; London, Yale University Press, 1995), p. 330.

3 Figes, Orlando. *A people's tragedy: the Russian Revolution, 1891–1924* (London, Cape, 1996), p. 182.

4 *Ibid.* pp. 47–48.

5 Roosevelt, Priscilla. *Life on the Russian country estate: a social and cultural history* (New Haven, CT; London, Yale University Press, 1995), pp. 327–328.

Chapter 14: A Musical Interlude

1 Graham, Stephen. *Russia in 1916* (London, Cassell, 1917), pp. 37–39.

2 *Ibid.* p. 44.

3 *Ibid.* p. 36.

4 *Ibid.* p. 42.

Chapter 15: Revolution

1 *The Times*, Nov 04, 1916.

2 Bruce Lockhart, R. H. *Memoirs of a British agent* (London; New York, Putnam, 1932; Barnsley, Pen and Sword Books/Frontline Books, 2011), p. 171.

3 *The Times*, Jan 29, 1917.

4 Figes, Orlando. *A people's tragedy: the Russian Revolution, 1891–1924* (London, Cape, 1996), p. 309.

5 Smith, Douglas. *Former people: the last days of the Russian aristocracy* (London, Macmillan, 2012), p. 70; Figes, Orlando. *A people's tragedy: the Russian Revolution, 1891–1924* (London, Cape, 1996), p. 312.

6 Jones, Stinton. *Russia in revolution: being the experiences of an Englishman in Petrograd during the upheaval* (Bristol, Chivers, 1992).

7 Figes, Orlando. *A people's tragedy: the Russian Revolution, 1891–1924* (London, Cape, 1996), p. 315.

8 Smith, Douglas. *Former people: the last days of the Russian aristocracy* (London, Macmillan, 2012), p. 70.

9 Figes, Orlando. *A people's tragedy: the Russian Revolution, 1891–1924* (London, Cape, 1996), pp. 307–353. Smith, Douglas. *Former people: the last days of the Russian aristocracy* (London, Macmillan, 2012), pp. 69–80.

10 Urch, Reginald Oliver Gilling. *We generally shoot Englishmen* (London, George Allen & Unwin, 1936), p. 42.

11 *Ibid.*

12 *Ibid.* p. 41.

13 Bruce Lockhart, R. H. *Memoirs of a British agent* (London; New York, Putnam, 1932; Barnsley, Pen and Sword Books/Frontline Books, 2011), pp. 169–170.

14 *The Blackwell encyclopaedia of the Russian Revolution*, edited by Harold Shukman (Oxford, Blackwell Reference, 1988), pp. 328–329.

15 Bruce Lockhart, R. H. *Memoirs of a British agent* (London; New York, Putnam, 1932; Barnsley, Pen and Sword Books/Frontline Books, 2011), p. 178.

16 *Ibid.*

17 Urch, Reginald Oliver Gilling. *We generally shoot Englishmen* (London, George Allen & Unwin, 1936), pp. 56–57.

18 *Ibid.* pp. 57–60.

19 Figes, Orlando. *A people's tragedy: the Russian Revolution, 1891–1924* (London, Cape, 1996), p. 330.

20 Anet, Claude. *La révolution russe, À Petrograd et aux armées (mars–mai 1917)* (Paris, Payot & cie., 1919), p. 56.

21 Browder, Robert Paul and Kerensky, Alexander. *The Russian Provisional Government, 1917: documents*, selected and edited by Robert Paul Browder and Alexander F. Kerensky (Stanford, CA, Stanford University Press, 1961), vol. II, p. 882.

22 Figes, Orlando. *A people's tragedy: the Russian Revolution, 1891–1924* (London, Cape, 1996), p. 380.

23 Anet, Claude. *La révolution russe, À Petrograd et aux armées (mars–mai 1917)* (Paris, Payot & cie., 1919).

24 Figes, Orlando. *A people's tragedy: the Russian Revolution, 1891–1924* (London, Cape, 1996), p. 447.

25 *Ibid.* p. 448.

26 *Ibid.* p. 462.

27 Steinberg, Mark D. *Voices of revolution, 1917*, documents translated by Marian Schwartz; documents compiled by Mark D. Steinberg, Zinaida Peregudova and Liubov Tiutiunnik (New Haven, CT; London, Yale University Press, 2001), pp. 98–99; Bunyan, James and Fisher, Harold, H. *The Bolshevik revolution, 1917–1918: documents and materials* (Stanford, CA, Stanford University Press, 1965), c.1934.

28 Radó, Sándor. *Guide-book to the Soviet Union*, compiled by A. Radó, issued by the Society for cultural relations of the

Soviet Union with Foreign Countries (New York, International Publishers Co., 1928).

29 Pitcher, Harvey J. *Witnesses of the Russian Revolution* (London, John Murray, 1994), p. 238.

30 Pasternak, Alexander and Slater, Ann Pasternak. *A vanished present: the memoirs of Alexander Pasternak*, edited and translated by Ann Pasternak Slater (Oxford, Oxford University Press, 1984), p. 205; Figes, Orlando. *A people's tragedy: the Russian Revolution, 1891–1924* (London, Cape, 1996), p. 497.

31 Bunyan, James and Fisher, Harold, H. *The Bolshevik revolution, 1917–1918: documents and materials* (Stanford, CA, Stanford University Press, 1965, *c.*1934), pp. 174–175.

32 Figes, Orlando. *A people's tragedy: the Russian Revolution, 1891–1924* (London, Cape, 1996), p. 497.

33 Bunyan, James and Fisher, Harold, H. *The Bolshevik revolution, 1917–1918: documents and materials* (Stanford, CA, Stanford University Press, 1965, *c.*1934), pp. 179–180.

34 Urch, Reginald Oliver Gilling. *We generally shoot Englishmen* (London, George Allen & Unwin, 1936), pp. 80–81.

35 Pasternak, Alexander and Slater, Ann Pasternak. *A vanished present: the memoirs of Alexander Pasternak*, edited and translated by Ann Pasternak Slater (Oxford, Oxford University Press, 1984), p. 181; p. 205.

36 Sayler, Oliver M. *Russia White or Red* (Boston, Little, Brown, and Company, 1919), p. 28.

37 Chamberlin, William Henry. *The Russian revolution, 1917–1921* (New York, The Macmillan Company, 1935).

38 moscowanglican.org.

39 Pasternak, Alexander and Slater, Ann Pasternak. *A vanished present: the memoirs of Alexander Pasternak*, edited and translated by Ann Pasternak Slater (Oxford, Oxford University Press, 1984), pp. 205–206.

40 *Ibid.* p. 208.

41 Zvereva, Svetlana G. *Alexander Kastalsky: his life and music* (Aldershot, Ashgate Publishing, 2003), p. 189.

42 Smith, Douglas. *Former people: the last days of the Russian aristocracy* (London, Macmillan, 2012), p. 112.

43 Radó, Sándor. *Guide-book to the Soviet Union*, compiled by A. Radó, issued by the Society for cultural relations of the Soviet Union with Foreign Countries, (New York, International Publishers Co., 1928).

44 Sayler, Oliver M. *Russia White or Red* (Boston, Little, Brown, and Company, 1919), p. 35.

45 *Ibid.*

46 Ransome, Arthur. *Six weeks in Russia in 1919* (London, George Allen & Unwin, 1919), p. 18.

47 Sayler, Oliver M. *Russia White or Red* (Boston, Little, Brown, and Company, 1919), p. 36.

48 Urch, Reginald Oliver Gilling. *We generally shoot Englishmen* (London, George Allen & Unwin, 1936), p. 83.

49 Sayler, Oliver M. *Russia White or Red* (Boston, Little, Brown, and Company, 1919), p. 113.

50 *Ibid.* p. 110.

Chapter 16: Red Moscow

1 Urch, Reginald Oliver Gilling. *We generally shoot Englishmen* (London, George Allen & Unwin, 1936), p. 127.

2 Bunyan, James and Fisher, Harold, H. *The Bolshevik revolution, 1917–1918: documents and materials* (Stanford, CA, Stanford University Press, 1965, *c.*1934), pp. 128–129.

3 *Ibid.* pp. 323–325.

4 *Ibid.* p. 543.

5 Urch, Reginald Oliver Gilling. *We generally shoot Englishmen* (London, George Allen & Unwin, 1936), pp. 97–98.

6 *Ibid.* p. 127.

7 Meyendorff, Stella Zoe Whishaw, Baroness. *Through terror to freedom: the dramatic story of an English woman's life and adventures in Russia, before, during & after the revolution* (London, Hutchinson & Co, 1929), p. 128.

8 Smith, Douglas. *Former people: the last days of the Russian aristocracy* (London, Macmillan, 2012), p. 118.

9 Bunyan, James. *Intervention, Civil War, and Communism in Russia, April–December 1918* (Baltimore, MD, Johns Hopkins University, Walter Hines Page School of International Relations, 1936), p. 190.

10 Figes, Orlando. *A people's tragedy: the Russian Revolution, 1891–1924* (London, Cape, 1996), p. 594.

11 Smith, Douglas. *Former people: the last days of the Russian aristocracy* (London, Macmillan, 2012), p. 76.

12 Urch, Reginald Oliver Gilling. *We generally shoot Englishmen* (London, George Allen & Unwin, 1936), p. 136.

13 *Ibid.*

14 Figes, Orlando. *A people's tragedy: the Russian Revolution, 1891–1924* (London, Cape, 1996), p. 528.

15 Bunin, Ivan. *Cursed days: a diary of Revolution*, translated from the Russian, with an introduction and notes by Thomas Gaiton Marullo (Chicago, Ivan R. Dee, 1998), pp. 53–54.

16 Colton, Timothy J. *Moscow: governing the socialist metropolis* (Cambridge, MA, Belknap Press of Harvard University Press, 1995), p. 118.

17 Figes, Orlando. *A people's tragedy: the Russian Revolution, 1891–1924* (London, Cape, 1996), p. 527.

18 *From a Russian diary, 1917–1920*, by an Englishwoman (London, John Murray, 1921), p. 125.

19 Colton, Timothy J. *Moscow: governing the socialist metropolis* (Cambridge, MA, Belknap Press of Harvard University Press, 1995), p. 110.

20 Tolstoy, V. P., Bibikova, I. M. and Cooke, Catherine. *Street art of the revolution: festivals and celebrations in Russia, 1918–1933*, edited by Vladimir Tolstoy, Irina Bibikova and Catherine Cooke (London, Thames and Hudson, 1990), p. 39.

21 Von Geldern, James. *Bolshevik festivals, 1917–1920* (Berkeley, CA; London, University of California Press, 1993), p. 95.

22 Tolstoy, V. P., Bibikova, I. M. and Cooke, Catherine. *Street art of the revolution: festivals and celebrations in Russia, 1918–1933*, edited by Vladimir Tolstoy, Irina Bibikova and Catherine Cooke (London, Thames and Hudson, 1990), p. 56.

23 Ransome, Arthur. *Six weeks in Russia in 1919* (London, George Allen & Unwin, 1919), p. 23.

24 *Ibid.* pp. 22–23.

Chapter 17: Flight

1 Smith, Douglas. *Former people: the last days of the Russian aristocracy* (London, Macmillan, 2012), p. 143.

2 Bunyan, James. *Intervention, Civil War, and Communism in Russia, April–December 1918* (Baltimore, MD, Johns Hopkins University, Walter Hines Page School of International Relations, 1936), p. 237.

3 Urch, Reginald Oliver Gilling. *We generally shoot Englishmen* (London, George Allen & Unwin, 1936), p. 189.

4 *Ibid.* p. 148.

5 *Ibid.* p. 145.

6 Pitcher, Harvey J. *Chekhov's leading lady: a portrait of the actress Olga Knipper* (London, John Murray, 1979), p. 219.

7 Schwarz, Boris. *Music and musical life in Soviet Russia, 1917–1970* (London, Barrie & Jenkins, 1972), p. 17.

8 Bunin, Ivan. *Cursed days: a diary of Revolution*, translated from the Russian, with an introduction and notes by Thomas Gaiton Marullo (Chicago, Ivan R. Dee, 1998), p. 54.

NOTES

9 Urch, Reginald Oliver Gilling. *We generally shoot Englishmen* (London, George Allen & Unwin, 1936), p. 139.

10 *The Times*, Feb 08, 1918; Meyendorff, Stella Zoe Whishaw, Baroness. *Through terror to freedom: the dramatic story of an English woman's life and adventures in Russia, before, during & after the revolution* (London, Hutchinson & Co, 1929), pp. 131–132.

11 Tsvetaeva, Marina. *Earthly signs: Moscow diaries, 1917–1922*, edited, translated, and with an introduction by Jamey Gambrell (New Haven, CT; London, Yale University Press, 2002), pp. 164–165.

12 Colton, Timothy J. *Moscow: governing the socialist metropolis.* (Cambridge, MA, Belknap Press of Harvard University Press, 1995), p. 124.

13 *The Blackwell encyclopaedia of the Russian Revolution*, edited by Harold Shukman (Oxford, Blackwell Reference, 1988).

14 Schwarz, Boris. *Music and musical life in Soviet Russia, 1917–1970* (London, Barrie & Jenkins, 1972), p. 17.

15 Eudin, Xenia Joukoff. 'Soviet National Minority Policies 1918–1921'. *Slavonic and East European Review. American Series*, vol. 2, no. 2, 1943, p. 37, JSTOR.

16 Eksteins, Modris. *Walking since daybreak: a story of Eastern Europe, World War II, and the heart of the twentieth century* (London, Papermac, 2000), p. 62.

17 Latvia Sūtniecība (U.S.)/Bilmanis, Alfred. *Latvian-Russian relations: documents*, compiled by Dr Alfred Bilmanis (Washington, DC, Latvian legation, 1944), p. 60.

18 Figes, Orlando. *A people's tragedy: the Russian Revolution, 1891–1924* (London, Cape, 1996), p. 526.

19 Kennard, Howard Percy. *The Russian peasant* (London, T. Werner Laurie, 1907), pp. 60–61.

20 Urch, Reginald Oliver Gilling. *We generally shoot Englishmen* (London, George Allen & Unwin, 1936), p. 238.

21 *Ibid.* pp. 238–239.

22 *From a Russian diary, 1917–1920*, by an Englishwoman (London, John Murray, 1921), p. 191.

23 Jarosy, Albert. 'Nicolas Medtner'. *The Listener*, vol. XVI, no. 401, 16 September, 1936.

Chapter 18: Riga 1919

1 Figes, Orlando. *A people's tragedy: the Russian Revolution, 1891–1924* (London, Cape, 1996), pp. 542–543.

2 The National Archives, ADM 137/1663.

3 Spekke, Arnolds. *History of Latvia: an outline*, translations from Latvian into English by H. Kundzins and others (Stockholm, M. Goppers, 1951), p. 346.

4 Silverlight, John. *The victors' dilemma: Allied intervention in the Russian Civil War* (London, Barrie & Jenkins, 1970), p. 294.

5 The National Archives, CAB 23/42.

6 *Ibid.* ADM 137/2488.

7 *The Times*, Dec 17, 1918.

8 The National Archives, ADM 137/1663.

9 *The Times*, Jan 02, 1919.

10 The National Archives, ADM 137/1664.

11 *Ibid.* CAB 23/42/20.

12 *Ibid.* ADM 137/1664.

13 *Ibid.* ADM 137/1663.

14 Bennett, Geoffrey. *Cowan's war: the story of British naval operations in the Baltic, 1918–1920* (London, Collins, 1964), pp. 48–49.

15 Popoff, George. *The city of the Red plague: Soviet rule in a Baltic Soviet town*, translated by Robin John (London, George Allen & Unwin Ltd, 1932), p. 45.

16 *Ibid.* pp. 49–51.

17 *Ibid.* pp. 136–138.

18 The National Archives, FO 608/185.

19 Schwarz, Boris. *Music and musical life in Soviet Russia, 1917–1970* (London, Barrie & Jenkins, 1972), p. 16.

20 Chaliapin, Feodor Ivanovich. *Pages from my life: an autobiography* (New York and London, 1927), p. 310.

21 Spekke, Arnolds. *History of Latvia: an outline*, translations from Latvian into English by H. Kundzins and others (Stockholm, M. Goppers, 1951), p. 348.

22 The National Archives, FO 608/185.

23 Popoff, George. *The city of the Red plague: Soviet rule in a Baltic Soviet town*, translated by Robin John (London, George Allen & Unwin Ltd, 1932), p. 87.

24 *Ibid.* p. 67.

25 Spekke, Arnolds. *History of Latvia: an outline*, translations from Latvian into English by H. Kundzins and others (Stockholm, M. Goppers, 1951), p. 348.

26 The National Archives, FO 608/185.

27 Spekke, Arnolds. *History of Latvia: an outline*, translations from Latvian into English by H. Kundzins and others (Stockholm, M. Goppers, 1951), p. 350.

28 Popoff, George. *The city of the Red plague: Soviet rule in a Baltic Soviet town*, translated by Robin John (London, George Allen & Unwin Ltd, 1932), pp. 332–335.

29 Tallents, Stephen G. *Man and boy* (London, Faber and Faber, 1943), pp. 309–312.

30 Du Parquet, Emmanuel Joseph Marie. *L'Aventure Allemande en Lettonie, etc.* (Paris, 1926), p. 73.

31 The National Archives, FO 608/185.

32 *Ibid.* ADM 137/1667.

Chapter 19: Libau 1919

1 Williamson, Gordon. *The Iron Cross: a history, 1813–1957* (Poole, Blandford Press, 1984), pp. 47–48.

2 Watson, H. A. G. *The Latvian republic* (London, George Allen & Unwin, 1965), p. 21.

3 Spekke, Arnolds. *History of Latvia: an outline*, translations from Latvian into English by H. Kundzins and others (Stockholm, M. Goppers, 1951), p. 347.

4 Kinvig, Clifford. *Churchill's crusade: the British invasion of Russia, 1918–1920* (London, Hambledon Continuum, 2006), p. 141.

5 Watson, H. A. G. *The Latvian republic* (London, George Allen & Unwin, 1965), pp. 53–54.

6 The National Archives, FO 608/185.

7 *Ibid.* ADM 137/1665.

8 *Ibid.* ADM 137/1671.

9 *Ibid.* ADM 137/1665.

10 *The Times*, Apr 22, 1919.

11 Watson, H. A. G. *The Latvian republic* (London, George Allen & Unwin, 1965), p. 99.

12 *Ibid.* p. 55.

13 The National Archives, ADM 137/1666.

14 *Ibid.* ADM 137/1667.

15 *Ibid.*

16 *Ibid.* FO 608/185.

17 Bane, Suda Lorena and Lutz, Ralph Haswell. *Organization of American Relief in Europe, 1918–1919, including negotiations leading up to the establishment of the Office* of *Director General of Relief at Paris by the Allied and associated powers.* Documents selected and edited by S. L. Bane and R. H. Lutz (Stanford University, Stanford University Press; London, Oxford University Press, 1943), p. 12.

18 Watson, H. A. G. *The Latvian republic* (London, George Allen & Unwin, 1965), p. 59.

19 Woodward, E. L. and Butler, Rohan. *Documents on British foreign policy, 1919–1939*, edited by E. L. Woodward and Rohan Butler, 1st series, 1919 (London, HMSO, 1949), vol. 3, p. 47.

20 *Ibid.* p. 52.
21 *Ibid.* p. 76.
22 The National Archives, ADM 137/1667.

Chapter 20: Berlin

1 Weitz, Eric D. *Weimar Germany: promise and tragedy* (Princeton, NJ; London, Princeton University Press, 2007), pp. 16–39.
2 Baedeker, Karl. *Berlin and its environs: handbook for travellers* (Leipzig, Karl Baedeker, 1923), p. 24.
3 Weitz, Eric D. *Weimar Germany: promise and tragedy* (Princeton, NJ; London, Princeton University Press, 2007), p. 2.
4 *Ibid.* p. 32.
5 Wietzorek, Paul. *Historic Berlin: pictures tell the story*, translation Rhett Griffith (Michael Imhof Verlag, 2008), p. 140.
6 Rabinavicius, Henrikas. 'The Fate of the Baltic Nations'. *The Russian Review*, vol. 3, no. 1, 1943, pp. 38–39, JSTOR.
7 Rutter, Owen. *The new Baltic states and their future: an account of Lithuania, Latvia and Estonia* (London, Methuen, 1925), p. 128.
8 Bennett, Geoffrey. *Cowan's war: the story of British naval operations in the Baltic, 1918–1920* (London, Collins, 1964), pp. 189–191.
9 Rutter, Owen. *The new Baltic states and their future: an account of Lithuania, Latvia and Estonia* (London, Methuen, 1925), p. 128.
10 Rabinavicius, Henrikas. 'The Fate of the Baltic Nations'. *The Russian Review*, vol. 3, no. 1, 1943, pp. 34–44, JSTOR.
11 Jelavich, Peter. *Berlin cabaret* (Cambridge, MA; London, Harvard University Press, 1993).
12 *Ibid.* p. 34.
13 Bessel, Richard. *Germany after the First World War* (Oxford, Clarendon Press, 1993), p. 221.
14 Weitz, Eric D. *Weimar Germany: promise and tragedy* (Princeton, NJ; London, Princeton University Press, 2007), p. 4.

15 Holden, Raymond. *The virtuoso conductors: the Central European tradition from Wagner to Karajan* (New Haven, CT; London, Yale University Press, 2005), pp. 40–51.

16 *Ibid.* p. 56.

17 *The Musical Times*, July 1908.

18 Holden, Raymond. *The virtuoso conductors: the Central European tradition from Wagner to Karajan* (New Haven, CT; London, Yale University Press, 2005), pp. 57–59.

19 Oehlmann, Werner. *Das Berliner Philharmonische Orchester* (Kassel; Basel; Tours; London, Bärenreiter-Verlag, 1974), pp. 45–56.

Chapter 21: America

1 Brown, Henry Collins. *Valentine's city of New York; a guide book, with six maps and one hundred and sixty full page pictures* (New York, Valentine's Manual, inc., 1920), pp. 110–111.

2 Brown, Henry Collins. *The city of New York* (New York, J. M. Ruston, 1917), p. 193.

3 Fucito, Salvatore and Beyer, Barnet J. *Caruso and the art of singing: including Caruso's vocal exercises and his practical advice to students and teachers of singing* (New York, Frederick A. Stokes, 1922), p. 139.

4 metopera.org.

5 Bos, Coenraad V. *The well-tempered accompanist*, as told to Ashley Pettis (Bryn Mawr, PA, T Presser Co., 1949), p. 52.

6 Mackrell, Judith. *Bloomsbury ballerina: Lydia Lopokova, imperial dancer and Mrs John Maynard Keynes* (London, Weidenfeld & Nicolson, 2008).

7 *New-York Tribune*, 12 April 1921, Library of Congress, Chronicling America.

8 *Times-Picayune*, New Orleans, 12 February 1921, p. 10.

9 *Ibid.* 20 February 1921, p. 42.

10 *Ibid.* 12 February 1921, p. 10.

11 Programme. Louisiana State Museum Historical Center Archives.

12 *New Orleans City Guide*, written and compiled by the Federal Writers' Project of the Works Progress Administration for the city of New Orleans (Boston, Houghton Mifflin, 1938), p. 320.

13 Programme. Louisiana State Museum Historical Center Archives.

14 *Times-Picayune*, New Orleans, 27 February 1921, p. 10.

15 *Ibid.*

16 Programme. *New-York Tribune*, 10 April, 1921, Library of Congress, Chronicling America.

17 Horowitz, Joseph. *Wagner nights: an American history* (Berkeley, CA; London, University of California Press, 1994), pp. 297–298.

18 Aldrich, Richard. *Concert life in New York, 1902–1923* (New York, Putnam, 1941), p. 621.

19 metopera.org.

20 *New-York Tribune*, 12 April 1921, Library of Congress, Chronicling America.

21 *The Evening World*, April 12, 1921, Library of Congress, Chronicling America.

22 *The Musician*, May 1921.

Chapter 22: Between the Wars

1 El-Tour, Anna, Madame. *Conseils sur l'art du chant* (La Haye (Hollande), J. Philip Kruseman; Paris, Durand & Cie., *c.*1934).

2 *The Musical Times*, April 1925.

3 *Ibid.* December 1937.

4 *The Sunday Times*, Jan 29, 1939.

5 Friedrich, Otto. *Before the deluge: a portrait of Berlin in the 1920s* (London, Michael Joseph, 1974), p. 175.

6 Drazin, Charles. *The Faber book of French cinema* (London, Faber and Faber, 2011), p. 178.

7 Everett, Susanne. *Lost Berlin* (New York, Gallery Books, 1979), p. 47.

8 Bessel, Richard. *Germany after the First World War* (Oxford, Clarendon Press, 1993), p. 93.

9 Weitz, Eric D. *Weimar Germany: promise and tragedy* (Princeton, NJ; London, Princeton University Press, 2007), pp. 207–209; Metzger, Rainer. *Berlin in the twenties: art and culture 1918–1933* (London, Thames and Hudson, 2007), p. 347.

10 Davies, R. E. G. *A history of the world's airlines*, with a foreword by Peter Masefield, and maps and charts by the author (London; New York, Oxford University Press, 1964), p. 25.

11 *Ibid.* pp. 21–38.

12 Davies, Ellen Chivers. *A wayfarer in Estonia, Latvia and Lithuania* (London, Methuen, 1937), p. 106.

13 *Baedeker's Russia 1914* by Karl Baedeker, David & Charles/George Allen & Unwin, 1971, p. 57.

14 Rutter, Owen. *The new Baltic states and their future: an account of Lithuania, Latvia and Estonia* (London, Methuen, 1925), p. 103.

15 Friedrich, Otto. *Before the deluge: a portrait of Berlin in the 1920s* (London, Michael Joseph, 1974), p. 85.

16 *The Musical Times*, July 1951.

17 Bradshaw, George. *Bradshaw's Continental Railway Guide 1913* (Oxford, Old House books, 2012 [London, Henry Blacklock & Co, 1913]), p. 473

18 *Jūrmala: nature and cultural heritage*, editor Laima Slava (Riga, Neptuns, c.2004), p. 119.

19 *The Times*, Jun 08, 1933.

Chapter 23: Finale

1 Charman, Terry. *Outbreak 1939: the world goes to war* (London, Virgin Books, 2009), p. xii.

2 Gardiner, Juliet. *The thirties: an intimate history* (London, Harper Press, 2010), p. 730.

3 *The Times*, Sep 26, 1938.

4 *Ibid.* Sep 28, 1938.

5 *Ibid.* Sep 29, 1938.

6 *Ibid.* Sep 30, 1938.

7 *Ibid.*

8 *The Times*, Sep 23, 1938; *The Times*, Sep 27, 1938; *The Times*, Sep 30, 1938.

9 *The Times*, Oct 01, 1938.

10 *Ibid.*

11 Charman, Terry. *Outbreak 1939: the world goes to war* (London, Virgin Books, 2009), p. 13.

12 *The Times*, Jul 01, 1939.

13 *Ibid.* Aug 25, 1939.

14 *Ibid.* Aug 24, 1939.

15 Charman, Terry. *Outbreak 1939: the world goes to war* (London, Virgin Books, 2009), p. 46.

16 *Ibid.* p. 58.

17 *The Times*, Aug 25, 1939.

18 *Ibid.* Sep 01, 1939.

19 *Ibid.* Sep 02, 1939.

20 *Ibid.* Aug 28, 1939.

21 Charman, Terry. *Outbreak 1939: the world goes to war* (London, Virgin Books, 2009), p. 61.

22 *Ibid.* p. 65.

23 *The Times*, Sep 02, 1939.

24 Ziegler, Philip. *London at war, 1939–1945* (London, Sinclair-Stevenson, 1995), p. 36.

25 Charman, Terry. *Outbreak 1939: the world goes to war* (London, Virgin Books, 2009), p. 183.

Chapter 24: Epilogue

1 Pact of Mutual Assistance Between Latvia and the Union of Soviet Socialist Republics, Article III. *Latvia in 1939–1942*

(Press Bureau of the Latvian Legation, Washington DC, 1942), p. 103.

2 Ezergailis, Andrew. *The holocaust in Latvia, 1941–1944: the missing center* (Riga, The Historical Institute of Latvia, in association with The United States Holocaust Memorial Museum, Washington, DC, 1996), pp. 37–39.

Select Bibliography

Abraham, Richard. *Alexander Kerensky: the first love of the revolution* (London, Sidgwick & Jackson, 1987).

Aldrich, Richard. *Concert life in New York, 1902–1923* (New York, Putnam, 1941).

Anet, Claude. *La révolution russe, À Petrograd et aux armées (mars–mai 1917)* (Paris, Payot & cie., 1919).

Baedeker, Karl. *The United States, with excursions to Mexico, Cuba, Porto Rico, and Alaska: handbook for travellers*, 4th rev. ed. (Leipzig, Karl Baedeker; London, T. Fisher Unwin, 1909).

Baedeker, Karl. *Le Sud-Est de la France du Jura à la Méditerranée y Compris la Corse* (Leipzig, Karl Baedeker, 1910).

Baedeker, Karl. *Berlin and its environs: handbook for travellers* (Leipzig, Karl Baedeker, 1912).

Baedeker, Karl. *Berlin and its environs: handbook for travellers* (Leipzig, Karl Baedeker, 1923).

Baedeker, Karl. *Germany: a handbook for railway travellers and motorists* (Leipzig, Karl Baedeker; London, George Allen & Unwin, 1936).

Baedeker's Russia 1914 by Karl Baedeker, David & Charles/George Allen & Unwin, 1971,

Bainbridge, Henry Charles. *Peter Carl Fabergé, goldsmith and jeweller to the Russian imperial court: his life and work*, with a foreword by Sacheverell Sitwell (London, Spring Books, 1966).

Bane, Suda Lorena and Lutz, R. H. *Organization of American Relief in Europe, 1918–1919, including negotiations leading up to the establishment of the Office of Director General of Relief at Paris by the Allied and associated powers*. Documents selected and edited by S. L. Bane and R. H. Lutz (Stanford University, Stanford University Press; London, Oxford University Press, 1943).

Bartlett, Rosamund. *Chekhov: scenes from a life* (London, Free Press, 2004).

Bartlett, Rosamund. 'Russian culture: 1801–1917', in Perrie, Maureen, Lieven, Dominic and Suny, Ronald Grigor (eds.), *The Cambridge history of Russia* (Cambridge, Cambridge University Press, 2006), Vol. II.

Bennett, Geoffrey. *Cowan's war: the story of British naval operations in the Baltic, 1918–1920* (London, Collins, 1964).

Bessel, Richard. *Germany after the First World War* (Oxford, Clarendon Press, 1993).

Bilmanis, Alfred. *A History of Latvia* (Princeton, NJ, Princeton University Press, 1951).

The Blackwell encyclopaedia of the Russian Revolution, edited by Harold Shukman (Oxford, Blackwell Reference, 1988).

Blume, Mary. *Côte d'Azur: inventing the French Riviera* (London, Thames and Hudson, 1992).

Borovsky, Victor. *Chaliapin: a critical biography* (London, Hamish Hamilton, 1988).

Bos, Coenraad V. *The well-tempered accompanist*, as told to Ashley Pettis (Bryn Mawr, PA, T Presser Co., 1949).

Bowen, José A., et al. 'Mengelberg'. *Grove Music Online. Oxford Music Online*. Oxford University Press.

Bowman, Linda. 'Russia's First Income Taxes: The Effects of Modernized Taxes on Commerce and Industry, 1885–1914'. *Slavic Review*, vol. 52, no. 2, 1993, pp. 256–282, JSTOR.

Bradshaw, George. *Bradshaw's Continental Railway Guide 1913* (Oxford, Old House books, 2012 [London, Henry Blacklock & Co, 1913]).

British documents on the origins of the War, 1898–1914, edited by G. P. Gooch and Harold Temperley (London, H. M. Stationery Office, 1929), vol. IV.

Browder, Robert Paul and Kerensky, Alexander. *The Russian Provisional Government, 1917: documents*, selected and edited by Robert Paul Browder and Alexander F. Kerensky (Stanford, CA, Stanford University Press, 1961), vol. II.

Brown, Henry Collins. *The city of New York* (New York, J. M. Ruston, 1917).

Brown, Henry Collins. *Valentine's city of New York; a guide book, with six maps and one hundred and sixty full page pictures* (New York, Valentine's Manual, inc., 1920).

Bruce Lockhart, R. H. *Memoirs of a British agent* (London; New York, Putnam, 1932; Barnsley, Pen and Sword Books/Frontline Books, 2011).

Brumfield, William C. *A history of Russian architecture*, text and photographs by William Craft Brumfield (Cambridge, Cambridge University Press, 1993).

Buchanan, George, Sir. *My mission to Russia and other diplomatic memories* (London, Cassell and Company Ltd, 1923), vol. I.

Bunin, Ivan. *Cursed days: a diary of Revolution*, translated from the Russian, with an introduction and notes by Thomas Gaiton Marullo (Chicago, Ivan R. Dee, 1998).

Bunyan, James. *Intervention, Civil War, and Communism in Russia, April–December 1918.* (Baltimore, MD, Johns Hopkins University, Walter Hines Page School of International Relations, 1936).

Bunyan, James and Fisher, Harold, H. *The Bolshevik revolution, 1917–1918: documents and materials* (Stanford, CA, Stanford University Press, 1965, c.1934).

Cahn, Peter. 'Frankfurt'. *Grove Music Online. Oxford Music Online*. Oxford University Press.

Chaliapin, Fyodor Ivanovich, Gorky, Maksim, Froud, Nina and Hanley, James. *Chaliapin: an autobiography as told to Maxim Gorky*, with supplementary correspondence and notes, compiled and edited by Nina Froud and James Hanley (London, Macdonald, 1968).

Chaliapin, Fyodor Ivanovich and Pierre, André. *Ma vie*, traduit du Russe par André Pierre (Paris, Albin Michel, 1932).

Chaliapin, Fyodor Ivanovich. *Pages from my life: an autobiography* (New York and London, 1927).

Chamberlain, Lesley. *Volga, Volga: a journey down Russia's great river* (London, Picador, 1995).

Chamberlin, William Henry. *The Russian revolution, 1917–1921* (New York, The Macmillan Company, 1935).

Charman, Terry. *Outbreak 1939: the world goes to war* (London, Virgin Books, 2009).

Colton, Timothy J. *Moscow: governing the socialist metropolis* (Cambridge, MA, Belknap Press of Harvard University Press, 1995).

Crawford, Elizabeth. *The women's suffrage movement: a reference guide, 1866–1928* (London, UCL Press/Taylor and Francis Group, 1999).

Davies, Ellen Chivers. *A wayfarer in Estonia, Latvia and Lithuania* (London, Methuen, 1937).

Davies, R. E. G. *A history of the world's airlines*, with a foreword by Peter Masefield, and maps and charts by the author (London; New York, Oxford University Press, 1964).

Dollinger, Philippe. *The German Hansa*, translated and edited by D. S. Ault and S. H. Steinberg (London, Macmillan, 1970).

Dowler, Wayne. *Russia in 1913* (DeKalb, IL, Northern Illinois University Press, 2010).

Drazin, Charles. *The Faber book of French cinema* (London, Faber and Faber, 2011).

Du Parquet, Emmanuel Joseph Marie. *L'Aventure Allemande en Lettonie, etc.* (Paris, 1926).

Eksteins, Modris. *Walking since daybreak: a story of Eastern Europe, World War II, and the heart of the twentieth century* (London, Papermac, 2000).

El-Tour, Anna, Madame. *Conseils sur l'art du chant* (La Haye (Hollande), J. Philip Kruseman; Paris, Durand & Cie., *c.*1934).

Ely, Christopher. 'The Origins of Russian Scenery: Volga River Tourism and Russian Landscape Aesthetics'. *Slavic Review*, vol. 62, no. 4, 2003, pp. 666–682, JSTOR.

Eudin, Xenia Joukoff. 'Soviet National Minority Policies 1918–1921'. *Slavonic and East European Review. American Series*, vol. 2, no. 2, 1943, pp. 31–55, JSTOR.

Everett, Susanne. *Lost Berlin* (New York, Gallery Books, 1979).

Ezergailis, Andrew. *The holocaust in Latvia, 1941–1944: the missing center* (Riga, The Historical Institute of Latvia, in association with The United States Holocaust Memorial Museum, Washington, DC, 1996).

Figes, Orlando. *A people's tragedy: the Russian Revolution, 1891–1924* (London, Cape, 1996).

Figes, Orlando. *Natasha's dance: a cultural history of Russia* (London, Allen Lane, 2002).

Fleming, John and Honour, Hugh. *The Penguin dictionary of decorative arts* (London, Penguin Books, 1979).

Friedrich, Otto. *Before the deluge: a portrait of Berlin in the 1920s* (London, Michael Joseph, 1974).

From a Russian diary, 1917–1920, by an Englishwoman (London, John Murray, 1921).

From Russia: French and Russian Master Paintings 1870–1925 from Moscow and St Petersburg, catalogue by Natalia Ardashnikova et al. (London, Royal Academy of Arts, 2008).

Fucito, Salvatore and Beyer, Barnet J. *Caruso and the art of singing: including Caruso's vocal exercises and his practical advice to students and teachers of singing* (New York, Frederick A. Stokes, 1922).

219

Gardiner, Juliet *The thirties: an intimate history* (London, Harper Press, 2010).

Gatrell, Peter. *Russia's First World War: a social and economic history* (Harlow, Pearson/Longman, 2005).

Gintners, Jānis. *Liepājas gadsimti* (Liepāja, Liepājas Muzejs, 2004).

Gordon, Peter and Doughan, David. *Dictionary of British women's organisations, 1825–1960* (London, Woburn Press, 2001).

Gorky, Maksim, Barratt, Andrew and Scherr, Barry. *Maksim Gorky: selected letters*, selected, translated, and edited by Andrew Barratt and Barry P. Scherr (Oxford, Clarendon Press, 1997).

Graham, Stephen. *Russia in 1916* (London, Cassell, 1917).

Grosa, Silvija. *Art Nouveau in Riga* (Riga, Jumava).

Gutmānis, Dāvis. *Liepāja* (Riga, Jumava, 2002).

Haward, Lawrence W. and Ring, Reinhard. 'Jaques-Dalcroze, Emile'. *Grove Music Online. Oxford Music Online.* Oxford University Press.

Henriksson, Anders. 'Riga', in Hamm, Michael F. (ed.), *The City in late imperial Russia* (Bloomington, IN, Indiana University Press, 1986).

Holden, Raymond. *The virtuoso conductors: the Central European tradition from Wagner to Karajan* (New Haven, CT; London, Yale University Press, 2005).

Horowitz, Joseph. *Wagner nights: an American history* (Berkeley, CA; London,

University of California Press, 1994).

Hubback, J. H. *Russian realities: being impressions gathered during some recent journeys in Russia* (London, John Lane, 1915).

Hudson, Kenneth. *Air travel: a social history* (Bath, Adams and Dart, 1972).

Hurd, Archibald. 'The Fleets of our Allies'. *The Quarterly Review* (London, John Murray, 1917).

Jarosy, Albert. 'Nicolas Medtner'. *The Listener*, vol. XVI, no. 401, 16 September 1936.

Jelavich, Peter. *Berlin cabaret* (Cambridge, MA; London, Harvard University Press, 1993).

Jones, Stinton. *Russia in revolution: being the experiences of an Englishman in Petrograd during the upheaval* (Bristol, Chivers, 1992).

Jūrmala: nature and cultural heritage, editor Laima Slava (Riga, Neptuns, *c.*2004).

Kaun, Alexander Samuel. *Maxim Gorky and his Russia* (London, Jonathan Cape, 1932).

Kennard, Howard Percy. *The Russian peasant* (London, T. Werner Laurie, 1907).

Kennard, Howard Percy and Heyking, A. Baron, *The Russian Year-Book for 1911* (London, Eyre and Spottiswoode, Ltd., 1911).

Kinvig, Clifford. *Churchill's crusade: the British invasion of Russia, 1918–1920* (London, Hambledon Continuum, 2006).

Kolbergs, Andris. *The story of Riga* (Riga, Jāņa sēta, 1999).

Kotkin, Stephen. *Stalin* (London, Allen Lane, an imprint of Penguin Books, 2014).

Latvia as a transit country Western Europe – Russia: Latvian ports and railways. [b.v.]: [b.i.], 1923.

Latvia in 1939–1942 (Washington, DC, Press Bureau of the Latvian Legation, 1942).

Latvia. Sūtniecība (U.S.)/Bilmanis, Alfred. *Latvian-Russian relations: documents,* compiled by Dr Alfred Bilmanis (Washington, DC, Latvian legation, 1944).

Library of Congress, Chronicling America.

Lodijensky, N. 'The Forests of Russia'. *Russia: its industries and trade/ Issued by order of State Secretary S. J. de Witte…minister of* finance (Russia, Ministerstvo finansov. Glasgow, Hay Nisbet, 1901).

Longford, Christine. *Making conversation* (London, Persephone Books, 2009).

Louisiana State Museum Historical Center Archives.

Mackrell, Judith. *Bloomsbury ballerina: Lydia Lopokova, imperial dancer and Mrs John Maynard Keynes* (London, Weidenfeld & Nicolson, 2008).

Masson Hall Archives EUA GD58, the University of Edinburgh.

McBriar, A. M. *Fabian socialism and English politics, 1884–1918* (London, Cambridge University Press, 1962).

McVeagh, Diana. 'Elgar, Sir Edward'. *Grove Music Online*. *Oxford Music Online*. Oxford University Press.

Metzger, Rainer. *Berlin in the twenties: art and culture 1918–1933*, picture edited by Christian Brandstätter (London, Thames and Hudson, 2007)..

Meyendorff, Stella Zoe Whishaw, Baroness. *Through terror to freedom: the dramatic story of an English woman's life and adventures in Russia, before, during & after the revolution* (London, Hutchinson & Co, 1929).

New Orleans City Guide, written and compiled by the Federal Writers' Project of the Works Progress Administration for the city of New Orleans (Boston, Houghton Mifflin, 1938).

Nikulin, Lev. 'Chaliapin: a reminiscence', in Chaliapin, Fyodor Ivanovich, Gorky, Maksim, Froud, Nina and Hanley, James. *Chaliapin: an autobiography as told to Maxim Gorky*, with supplementary correspondence and notes, compiled and edited by Nina Froud and James Hanley (London, Macdonald, 1968).

Oehlmann, Werner. *Das Berliner Philharmonische Orchester* (Kassel; Basel; Tours; London, Bärenreiter-Verlag, 1974).

Official history (naval and military) of the Russo-Japanese war (London, H. M. Stationery Office, 1920).

Överdådets konst II, The Art of Extravagance II: Kostymer från Diaghilevs Ryska Baletten I Paris (Dansmuseet Stockholm, 2004).

Pascall, Robert. 'Knorr, Iwan'. *Grove Music Online*. *Oxford Music Online*. Oxford University Press.

Pascall, Robert. 'Stockhausen'. *Grove Music Online*. *Oxford Music Online*. Oxford University Press.

Pastaigas Liepājā: Pilsētas 370 Gadu Jubilejā (Liepāja, Kaste, 1995).

Pasternak, Alexander and Slater, Ann Pasternak. *A vanished present: the memoirs of Alexander Pasternak*, edited and translated by Ann Pasternak Slater (Oxford, Oxford University Press, 1984).

Peacock, Netta. *The Russian Year-Book for 1915* (London, Eyre and Spottiswoode, Ltd., 1915).

Pitcher, Harvey J. *Chekhov's leading lady: a portrait of the actress Olga Knipper* (London, John Murray, 1979).

Pitcher, Harvey J. *Muir & Mirrielees: the Scottish partnership that became a household name in Russia* (Cromer, Swallow House Books, 1994).

Pitcher, Harvey J. *Witnesses of the Russian Revolution* (London, John Murray, 1994).

Plakans, Andrejs. *Historical Dictionary of Latvia*, 2nd ed. (Lanham, MD, Scarecrow Press, 2008).

Polonsky, Rachel. *Molotov's magic lantern: a journey in Russian history* (London, Faber and Faber, 2010).

Popoff, George. *The city of the Red plague: Soviet rule in a Baltic Soviet town*, translated by Robin John (London, George Allen & Unwin Ltd, 1932).

Rabinavicius, Henrikas. 'The Fate of the Baltic Nations'. *The Russian Review*, vol. 3, no. 1, 1943, pp. 34–44, JSTOR.

Radó, Sándor. *Guide-book to the Soviet Union*, compiled by A. Radó, issued by the Society for cultural relations of the Soviet Union with Foreign Countries (New York, International Publishers Co., 1928).

Ransome, Arthur. *Six weeks in Russia in 1919* (London, George Allen & Unwin, 1919).

Raun, Toivo U. 'The Revolution of 1905 in the Baltic Provinces and Finland'. *Slavic Review*, vol. 43, no. 3, 1984, pp. 453–467, JSTOR.

Reich, Nancy, B. 'Schumann, Clara'. *Grove Music Online*. *Oxford Music Online*. Oxford University Press.

SELECT BIBLIOGRAPHY

Reid, Louis Arnaud *Yesterday's today: a journey into philosophy*, edited by Nicholas Reid (Canberra, Samizdat Press, 2013).

Robinson, Jane. *Bluestockings: the remarkable story of the first women to fight for an education* (London, Penguin Books, 2010).

Roosevelt, Priscilla. *Life on the Russian country estate: a social and cultural history* (New Haven, CT; London, Yale University Press, 1995).

Ross, Edward Alsworth. *Russia in upheaval* (New York, The Century Company, 1918, London, T. Fisher Unwin, 1919).

Rutter, Owen. *The new Baltic states and their future: an account of Lithuania, Latvia and Estonia* (London, Methuen, 1925).

Salmon, Patrick. *Scandinavia and the great powers 1890–1940* (Cambridge, Cambridge University Press, 2002).

Sanborn, Joshua A. *Imperial apocalypse: the great war and the destruction of the Russian empire* (Oxford, Oxford University Press, 2014).

Sayler, Oliver M. *Russia White or Red* (Boston, Little, Brown, and Company, 1919).

Sayler, Oliver Martin. *The Russian Theatre* (New York, Brentano's Publishers, 1922).

Schmidt, Albert J. *The architecture and planning of classical Moscow: a cultural history* (Philadelphia, PA, American Philosophical Society, 1989).

Schwarz, Boris. *Music and musical life in Soviet Russia, 1917–1970* (London, Barrie & Jenkins, 1972).

Silverlight, John. *The victors' dilemma: Allied intervention in the Russian Civil War* (London, Barrie & Jenkins, 1970).

Smith, Douglas. *Former people: the last days of the Russian aristocracy* (London, Macmillan, 2012).

Sollohub, Edith. *The Russian Countess: escaping revolutionary Russia* (Exeter, Impress Books, 2009).

Solzhenitsyn, Alexander. *August 1914*, translated by Michael Glenny (London, The Bodley Head Ltd, 1972).

Sondhaus, Lawrence. *The Great War at sea: a naval history of the First World War* (Cambridge, Cambridge University Press, 2014).

Spekke, Arnolds. *History of Latvia: an outline*, translations from Latvian into English by H. Kundzins and others (Stockholm, M. Goppers, 1951).

Stanislavsky, Constantin. *My Life in Art*, translated from the Russian by J. J. Robbins (London, Geoffrey Bles, 1924).

Steinberg, Mark D. *Voices of revolution, 1917*, documents translated by Marian Schwartz; documents compiled by Mark D. Steinberg, Zinaida Peregudova, and Liubov Tiutiunnik (New Haven; London, Yale University Press, 2001).

Stone, Norman. *The eastern front, 1914–1917* (London, Hodder and Stoughton, 1975).

Tallents, Stephen G. *Man and boy* (London, Faber and Faber, 1943).

The Times.

Times-Picayune.

Tolstoy, V. P., Bibikova, I. M. and Cooke, Catherine. *Street art of the revolution: festivals and celebrations in Russia, 1918–1933*, edited by Vladimir Tolstoy, Irina Bibikova and Catherine Cooke (London, Thames and Hudson, 1990).

Troyat, Henri. *La vie quotidienne en Russie au temps du dernier tsar* (Paris, Hachette, 1959).

Tsvetaeva, Marina. *Earthly signs: Moscow diaries, 1917–1922*, edited, translated, and with an introduction by Jamey Gambrell (New Haven, CT; London, Yale University Press, 2002).

University of Edinburgh Journal, Summer Number 1930, vol. III.

Urch, Reginald Oliver Gilling. *We generally shoot Englishmen* (London, George Allen & Unwin, 1936).

Von Geldern, James. *Bolshevik festivals, 1917–1920* (Berkeley, CA; London, University of California Press, 1993).

Washburn, Stanley. *The Russian campaign: April to August, 1915* (London, Andrew Melrose Ltd., 1915).

Watson, H. A. G. *The Latvian republic* (London, George Allen & Unwin, 1965).

Weitz, Eric D. *Weimar Germany: promise and tragedy* (Princeton, NJ; London, Princeton University Press, 2007).

Westwood, J. N. *A history of Russian railways* (London, Allen & Unwin, 1964).

Wietzorek, Paul. *Historic Berlin: pictures tell the story*, translation Rhett Griffith (Michael Imhof Verlag, 2008).

Williams, Harold. *Russia of the Russians* (London, Pitman & Sons, 1914).

Williams, Robert C. 'Russians in Germany: 1900–1914'. *Journal of Contemporary History*, vol. 1. no. 4, 1966, pp. 121–149, JSTOR.

Williamson, Gordon. *The Iron Cross: a history, 1813–1957* (Poole, Blandford Press, 1984).

Wood, Ruth Kedzie. *The tourist's Russia* (London, Andrew Melrose, 1912).

Woodward, E. L. and Butler, Rohan. *Documents on British foreign policy, 1919–1939*, edited by E. L. Woodward and Rohan Butler, 1st series, vol. 3 1919 (London, HMSO, 1949).

Worrall, Nick. *The Moscow Art Theatre* (London, Routledge, 1996).

Wortman, Richard. *Scenarios of power: myth and ceremony in Russian monarchy* (Princeton, NJ; Chichester, Princeton University Press, 2000), vol. II.

Ziegler, Philip. *London at war, 1939–1945* (London, Sinclair-Stevenson, 1995).

Zvereva, Svetlana G. *Alexander Kastalsky: his life and music* (Aldershot, Ashgate Publishing, 2003).